A Christian View of Money

A Christian
View of Money

Celebrating God's Generosity

(4th edition)

Mark L. Vincent,
Matthew M. Thomas,
and Zachary L. Vincent

WIPF & STOCK · Eugene, Oregon

A CHRISTIAN VIEW OF MONEY
Celebrating God's Generosity (4th edition)

Wipf & Stock
An Imprint of Wipf and Stock Publishers
199 W. 8th Ave., Suite 3
Eugene, OR 97401

www.wipfandstock.com

PAPERBACK ISBN: 978-1-4982-9318-1
HARDCOVER ISBN: 978-1-4982-9320-4
EBOOK ISBN: 978-1-4982-9319-8

Manufactured in the U.S.A.

Contents

From the Original Edition

IN OVER TWENTY-FIVE YEARS of working with money—the second most recurring theme in the Bible, I have found nothing more lacking than a truly helpful Christian viewpoint and spirit of giving.

This is perplexing because those who seek to live the life of serious discipleship and thus stewardship know that God is, above all else, a loving and giving God. God gave us a Savior, gave us the Scriptures, gave us the church, all as a part of divine creation—and yes, then gave us dominion over it all.

Beyond all this, men and women were created in God's very own image, which highlights the dilemma of our day. Rather than being generous, outgoing, committed, giving Christians, we find ourselves co-opted by a materialistic consumer culture that leads to our grabbing, holding on to, and protecting. We thus miss experiencing the great joy, justice and generosity of God in giving.

It is a great gift that Mark L. Vincent has written in a timely, helpful way, two very important books. *A Christian View of Money* provides the essential theological undergirding to working with money. The companion congregational manual, *Teaching a Christian View of Money*, is an equally compelling and very practical tool and guide to the marvelous *The Giving Project* that we so desperately need at this crucial hour in history. I feel that these are precisely the helping hands we have been looking for.

Thanks be to God!

—Don McClanen
Ministry of Money

ANABAPTISTS HAVE LONG UNDERSTOOD that how one lives, rather than what one says, is the most accurate description of what one believes. This is particularly true in the case of a Christian's use of money. Mark L. Vincent's *A Christian View of Money* is just the tool needed to make what we say we believe about money a reality in our daily lives. This package of material not only presents us with the blunt facts about the power of money and the biblical mandate for its use by God's people, but also a blueprint for individual and congregational change.

I am personally delighted in his presentation of God's work as a model of our stewardship. The theological foundation for A Christian's view of money is so clearly stated here that it could profitably be used as a new believer's guide to faith and doctrine. The summary statement of Christian beliefs about money (Appendix 3) for example, could well be the basis for every baptismal vow.

A word of warning is in order. Those looking for a guilt-reducing treatment or accommodation with cultural values will be disappointed in Vincent's refual to bless either avarice or accumulation. Likewise, those looking for mere information will be challenged by his clear direction for change. This is serious material designed to bring serious changes in our lives of stewardship, and will inevitably lead some of us to nothing less than conversion.

—Lynn Miller
   Author, *Firstfruits Living*

Author's Preface

MONEY HAS A GOD-LIKE power. I think about it a lot. How and when I might get more of it. What I will do with it once I get it. How much of it I want to share. How much I want to keep for myself. What I would do with it if I suddenly came into a large amount. Money consumes my waking moments and shows up in my dreams.

Even when I do not think about currency, credit cards, checking accounts or investments, I wonder about good prices on automobiles, clothing, and generic medications. For more than sixteen years I worried about my wife's health as she battled cancer, and all the tremendous costs involved. Then I worried final expenses, how to gather and dispense her estate, and whether the last medical bill had actually come in and been paid. I try to keep my taxes down; improve energy-saving measures in my home; and seek cost-effectives ways to travel from point A to point B.

Because of money's god-like power, a group of Norther American denominations developed called "The Giving Project: growing faithful stewards in the church." The purpose was to discern a set of Christian beliefs and practices regarding money, and then to develop methods to teach those beliefs and practices.

The initial publication of this volume covered the first part of the project, discerning beliefs about money. The second part—the methodology—was originally published as a three-ring binder, and now exists as a web-portal in several church traditions, updated to reflect the original doctoral research developed by Rev.

Barbara Fullerton after working with the material for more than ten years with Canadian congregations. One example of the updated methodology is the portal developed by the Metropolitan Chicago Synod of the ELCA (www.OpenHandsOpenHearts.com). These sites provide resources for congregations that choose to ask and answer two important questions:

> What do we need to do?
> What are we willing to do?

Distribution of this book, now the fourth edition, originally published for Mennonite congregations, exceeded everyone's expectations. We issue the fourth edition believing the conversation is far from over.

In preparing this edition, I sought the help of two more persons, younger adults both, helping me make sure the discussion items were updated and reflected current economic realities in North America. We also wanted to do a close read of the copy, keeping it updated now that this book has a twenty year history. So, I offer my thanks to Rev. Matthew M. Thomas, and Rev. Zach Vincent, for their assistance in pulling this together. Without them this volume would not be ready.

So many people have contributed to this work, not just at its inception when we conducted focus groups all across North America, but in the twenty-three years since, in congregations and among congregational leaders all over the world. What you read here grows from thousands of hours of conversation among people what want to live faithful Christian lives with their pocketbooks. It is the fruit of their work far more than mine.

This fourth edition is dedicated to my spouse of thirty-two years and Zach Vincent's mother, our beloved Lorie, now dwelling with God.

—Mark L. Vincent

Project Director for The Giving Project (formerly)
CEO, Design Group International
Kohler, WI
December 2016

Great and glorious Lord,

May the words of this book grow out of your words. Open the hearts of those who read it so that they carefully consider whether their use of money reflects your generous gift of grace. Make these printed words an instrument of your reign. In the strong name of Jesus, amen.

1

From the Beginning

CHRISTIANITY HAS A LONG history of describing how believers ought to use their money, including how they might continue in generosity. We want newcomers and youth to readily identify and embrace Christian beliefs about money. We need long-standing Christians to be more articulate about these beliefs, and these beliefs must be at the very heart of our faith because the link between faith and practice runs a strong current through North American wallets. Christians need to preserve and increase faithful use of money in order to better represent the generosity of Christ to a lost and broken world. Here are some examples, starting with one from the life of Jesus. Consider pausing for reflection as you read each one.

Example 1—A widow's offering (Luke 21:1-4)

Later in his ministry, Jesus observed people bringing financial gifts to the temple treasury. He watched wealthy people put in their gifts, and then saw a poor widow put in two copper coins. Then Jesus said, "This poor widow has put in more than all the others. All these people gave their gifts out of their wealth; but she out of her poverty put in all she had to live on" (Luke 21:3-4, NIV).

It is easy to turn this passage into a teaching on proportional giving. But Jesus did not bless the widow for giving proportionally more than wealthier ones did. Rather, he blessed her for giving out of their need, and for giving even when she had need. She gave all her resources as an act of worship to God, in contrast to those who gave from what was left over.

Example 2—The church's first fund drive (2 Cor. 8-9)

The Jerusalem Christians suffered the greatest of all first-century persecutions. Cut off from the jobs and economic assistance, they became destitute community. When famine ravaged the Mediterranean area at the same time, the apostle Paul instituted a fund-raising campaign, the framework of which churches use today in the gathering and dispensing of funds: "Each of you must give as you have made up your mind, not reluctantly or under compulsion, for God loves a cheerful giver. And God is able to provide you with every blessing in abundance, so that by always having enough of everything, you may share abundantly in every good work. As it is written, "He scatters abroad, he gives to the poor; his righteousness endures forever'" (2 Cor. 9:7-9 NRSV).

Example 3—Thoughts from earlier centuries

Ancient Christian writers wrote little about money, stewardship, tithing, materialism, or economic policy directly. It was not that they were not concerned about these matters, but their theology already covered the topics: Christians who have wealth above their basic needs ought to share it with those who have less. Doing so is an act of worship to Christ, and demonstrates trust in him.

> "Men would not be lovers of money unless they thought that their excellence depended on their wealth" (St. Augustine).[1]

> "Employ your riches with kindly devotion, and thus root out evil from your hearts. All that has value in your lives you must concentrate in the persons of the poor, and so

---

1. Nola, *Ancient Christian Writers,* 147.

anoint your heads with devoted giving" (St. Paulinus of Nola).[2]

Example 4—Citizens of another kingdom

Menno Simmons is best known as the church leader who assembled the persecuted and scattered Anabaptist community into a real church. He had a lot to say about money, wealth, possessions, and stewardship:

> "Our way of behaving is not . . . focused on perishable money or property . . . The born-again have a spiritual King over them [whose] name is Christ Jesus . . . Their citizenship is in heaven and they use the lower creations like eating, drinking, clothing, housing, with gratitude to meet their basic needs, to maintain their own life and to be able to serve their fellow human beings . . . Material increase is a gift of God to his children. Such goods are to be used wisely and sparingly for oneself and one's family. Any excess earned is to be shared with those in need, first with those of the household of faith (Galatians 6:10), and then with others in need."[3]

Example 5—Twentieth-century writings

1. In 1964, a Mennonite named A. Grace Wenger developed a Bible study on stewardship. *Stewards of the Gospel*, Ms. Wenger boldly wrote,

"No one can buy his way out of responsibility by giving money, no matter how generously he gives. Every area of a Christian's being belongs to God as surely as every part of a slave's person belonged to the master who had purchased them in the marketplace. Not only the fraction a Christian gives, but every cent that they keep, is

2. Ibid., 326.
3. Redekop, et al., *Anabaptist/Mennonite Faith and Economics*, 42.

God's. The Creator owns not one day of the week, but seven. A Christian's worship, certainly, but also his work and recreation, their getting and spending, their visiting and entertaining, must be done as unto the Lord."[4]

2. In 1983 the Mennonite Church General Board followed its 1955 declaration on wealth-seeking. (See Recommendation G. "Declaration of Commitment in Respect to Christian Separation and Nonconformity to the World," Item 2, "Attitude Toward Possessions.")[5] with the statement "A Call to Faithful Stewardship."[6]

3. *Baby boomers and giving:* In the early 1990s Gene Getz, a pastor in the Bible church tradition and a prolific author, wrote an elaborate work called *A Biblical Theology of Material Possessions.* The introduction describes directions of stewardship as the "baby-boomer" generation becomes the dominant force in church life:

> "Often designated as 'baby-boomers'—people born during the ten-to-twelve-year period following World War II—they have probably become the most materialistically oriented group of people in the 200 years of American history. For instance, researchers have discovered that baby boomers give almost nothing to any form of charity . . .
>
> "This mentality has also become a part of the Christian community. Some estimate that evangelical Christians give an average of only 2 percent of their income to further the kingdom of God. Since this statistic includes approximately 15 percent of those in the evangelical community who give at least 10 percent or more of their income, it is easy to conclude that Christian baby

---

4. Wenger, *Stewards of the Gospel,* 12.

5. *Proceedings,* Mennonite Church General Assembly, August 1-7, 1983, pp. 33, 34.

6. *Proceedings,* Mennonite General Conference, August 23-25, 1955, pp. 26, 27, 28.

boomers differ very little from their secular counter-
parts. They, too, give next to nothing . . .

"Because economic times had been very good over the
years, many Christians had been giving—primarily
when the need arose—out of what was 'left over,' rather
than out of what was set aside regularly as firstfruits. To
be more specific, the majority of Christians attending
our church (and other churches) were not regular, systematic, and proportional givers. God's work was not a
budget item—and, generally speaking, had never been.
Consequently, when they felt the economic crunch,
they had very little left over—virtually no excess to give.
It took everything they were earning to handle their
indebtedness—on their homes and their cars—and, in
many instances, on a number of items that were considered investments in the pure enjoyment of life . . .

"The majority of evangelical believers in our society are
not walking in the will of God in relationship to their
material possessions."[7]

4. *A statement of confession:* Two Mennonite denominations
came together in 1995 to contemporize their confession of
faith. The article on stewardship (21) states:

"We acknowledge that God as Creator is Owner of all
things. In the Old Testament , the Sabbath year and the
Jubilee year were practical expressions of the belief that
the land is God's and the people of Israel belong to God.
Jesus, at the beginning of his ministry, announced the
year of the Lord's favor, often identified with Jubilee.
Through Jesus the poor heard good news captives were
released, the blind saw, and the oppressed went free.
The first church in Jerusalem put Jubilee into practice
by preaching the gospel, healing the sick, and sharing
possessions. Other early churches shared financially
with those in need . . .

"As stewards of money and possessions, we are to live
simply, practice mutual aid within the church, uphold

7. Getz, *A Biblical Theology of Material Possessions,* 14–15.

economic justice, and give generously and cheerfully. As persons dependent on God's providence, we are not to be anxious about the necessities of life, but to seek first the kingdom of God. We cannot be true servants of God and let our lives be ruled by desire for wealth," . . .

"In the commentary on Article 21, it is noted that "[the Mennonite] tradition of simple living is rooted not in frugality for its own sake, but in dependence on God, the Owner of everything, for our material needs. We depend on God's gracious gifts for food and clothing, for our salvation, and for life itself. We do not need to hold on tight to money and possessions, but can share what God has given us. The practice of mutual aid is a part of sharing God's gifts so that no one in the family of faith will be without the necessities of life. Whether through community of goods or other forms of financial sharing, mutual aid continues the practice of Israel in giving special care to widows, orphans, aliens, and others in economic need (Deuteronomy 24:17-22). Tithes and firstfruit offerings were also a part of this economic sharing (Deuteronomy 26; compare Matthew 23:23) . . .

"We are to seek first and reign of God and to cease from consumerism, unchecked competition, overburdened productivity, greed, and possessiveness."[8]

Beliefs about money are part of the core Christian doctrines that transcend

the conservative/liberal or sacred/secular labels. People of nearly every Christian denomination, and even of many other religions, would say, "Amen. This is truth. This is what God expects." Where such a broad spectrum of affirmation can be found, it is wise to pay attention.

In light of that truth, Christians are called to follow Christ in a life of discipleship. A significant part of that discipleship is the faithful use of all the resources of which God has made us stewards. All these resources, as well as our lives, are entrusted to us to

---

8. *Confession of Faith in a Mennonite Perspective*, 77–79. The complete confessional statement and commentary is reprinted in Appendix 4.

use for the glory of God, for the furtherance of his kingdom and for the benefit of others.

This Call to Faithful Stewardship recognizes the pressures of our world to influence Christians to conform to its materialistic, accumulative, and consumptive values. Thus there is a need for the Church to call Christians to live by the teachings of Christ and his Word as faithful stewards.

This is a call to the Church to give special attention to faithful stewardship in the following ways:

A CALL TO RECEIVE GRATEFULLY

1. That all Christians recognize and acknowledge God as the Owner and Giver of all they are and all they have.

A CALL TO MANAGE FAITHFULLY

2. That all Christians adopt modest standards of living.

3. That all Christians be good stewards of the resources that they use (spending, borrowing, investing, saving, insurance, business, etc.)

A CALL TO SHARE GENEROUSLY

4. That all Christians rediscover and adopt the firstfruits tithe as a minimum standard for proportionate giving.

5. That all Christians volunteer a portion of their time and their abilities for the service in the Church at home and/or abroad.

6. That all Christians plan for the final distribution of their resources by writing wills and including the church along with family members.

2 _____

The Power of Money

*Belief: Because money has a godlike strength, our earning
and use of money communicate our values.*

MONEY IS GOD-LIKE FOR at least seven reasons. Small 'g,' but god-
like nevertheless.

1. *It outlives you.* Money was here before you, and it will be here
   after you pass away.

2. *Its circle of influence is greater.* Money goes places you can't go
   and touches people you cannot reach.

3. *Money is mysterious.* Its properties, impact and behavior
   cannot fully be described by anyone—even Alan Greenspan,
   head of the Federal Reserve Board of the United States from
   1897-2006. Mr. Greenspan always hedges his bets, "The
   economy could do this. Then again, it could do that," he says.
   Janet Yellen, head of the Federal Reserve Board of the United
   States since 2014 said, "As always . . . the economic outlook is
   uncertain."[1] No economist claims complete knowledge.

4. *Money lives among the things we are tempted to worship.* If
   money lives longer, has greater power, and is shrouded in
   mystery, it begins to sound like a god.

1. Accessed from the Wall Street Journal website on November 12, 2015;
www.wsj.com/briefly/BL-263B-5201.

5. *Money mimics everything promised in the New Jerusalem.* The Christian's eternal reward includes no crying, plentiful feasts, and beautiful housing. With money, we purchase a virtually real imitation. It might not be a wedding feast of the Lamb, but for $11.99 you eat all you want at Golden Corral or dinner (and fill up a take home box for $1.99 so the feast continues on into tomorrow). Maybe not a heavenly mansion, but you can buy a home in a gated community.

6. *It is an instrument you wield.* This verb "wield" describes the action of a sword and a scalpel. A sword is a tool of destruction, a scalpel an agent of healing. Money can do either, and sometimes both at the same time.

7. *Everything can be economized.* Does my church want to establish another congregation or send a missionary? There is an economic cost. Do I want a graduate degree? Money again. Do I hope to treat my wife to a wedding anniversary holiday? It's not free. What about repairing the environment? Money. Money. Money. Every noble intention has economic implications (See Appendix 5 for two more reasons money has a god-like power).

We dare not overlook this god-like power of money. Dreaming about making a fortune replaces prayer and devotion to God. Believing it fixes what we think is wrong grants it god-like power over our souls.

The point is this: handling money is a creative act, a work of art. While we intend something beautiful, we always risk creating disaster instead. Either way, we set economic activity in motion. We hold this god-like thing in our hands. In choosing our intentions for money—whether good or bad—we must first decide whether or not money will rule us.

As Paul writes in the first letter to Timothy, "We brought nothing into the world, so that we can take nothing out of it; but if we have food and clothing, we will be content with these. But those who want to be rich fall into temptation and are trapped by many senseless and harmful desires that plunge people into ruin and destruction. For the love of money is a root of all kinds of evil, and in their eagerness to be rich some have wandered away from the faith and pierced themselves with many pains" (1 Timothy 6:7-10 NRSV).

Principle 1: Contented people know the difference between need and desire.

Sometimes a desire will be the same as a need. We all desire adequate nutrition, health, safety, intimacy, meaningful work, shelter, self-worth. We also need these things. God knows that. The trick is to discern when desire blocks God's access to us. When what we want gets between us and God, or someone else has to do without their need because we fulfilled our desire, we have embraced the notion of entitlement and forgotten that all we have is a gift from God. Desires are things without which we can still be content, if we have God. I can call myself contented if, when my desire is not filled, I don't assume that God has abandoned me. The error is not in wanting something, but in the mistaken belief that fulfilled desire is the only path to contentment.

Contented people know, with Paul, that they cannot take anything out of this world, and that they can be satisfied with meeting basic needs. Paul discourages believers from assuming that Christianity means automatic financial prosperity.

In earlier verses of 1 Timothy 6, Paul described the kind of people who cannot discern need and desire:

a. *They give up on the teachings of Jesus and the body of doctrinal instruction that comes from it* (v. 3). It is not so much that they stop believing in Jesus as their Savior, but they do stop letting the gospel collide with their lifestyle and bring change. Now their lifestyle choices determine their response to the gospel instead of the other way around. They become arrogant and fail to take into consideration God's purposes (v. 4). Thus . . .

b. *They take an unhealthy interest in controversies and quarrels about words* (v. 4). Some North American churches are polarized by politics, focusing their congregational life around whatever heated issue they choose to make central to Christian faith. Other churches are little more than social clubs who gather to talk about faith, but present little challenge to actually live out its meaning. Churches like these hinder people from ministry. Why? Because freeing someone to minister means being challenged to do ministry oneself! And being challenged to minister reminds people of the other gods in their life. For many North Americans one of those gods in money.

c. *They might even degenerate all the way into thinking their skewed understanding of godliness leads to financial prosperity* (v. 5). Though early Wisdom Literature (for example, some of the Proverbs) connects prosperity with faithfulness, Paul cautions new Christians from jumping on the movement in anticipation of material gain. God does not promise a birthright that includes a large house with a luxury coupe in the garage and a six-figure bank account. If believers think economic gain should come from godliness, then they miss out on the greater gain of remaining content with needs being met, and using additional prosperity in generous ways to exalt God.

d. *They sometimes stop just distorting faith and end up abandoning it altogether* (v. 10). Perhaps people are more honest when they finally admit that money and the gospel compete with each other, but doing so makes their idolatry complete. They prove Jesus' words in Matthew 6:24, "You cannot serve God and wealth" (NRSV). They put all future hope in their ability to earn or spend, instead of in the saving grace of Jesus.

Christians can get just as worried about upward mobility as their neighbor. Such concerns limit our creativity to live generously. Money tempts us to abandon the gospel for one reason: We allow its godlike power to take God's place. J.R. Burkholder said it well in a 1974 article in *Gospel Herald*: "Money can indeed be a servant, but it is a dangerous servant.

It is a servant with such amazing potentialities that it requires a master big enough to control it, or else the roles may be reversed."[2]

Principle 2: "We are spirits in a material world."

The rock musician Sting once recorded a song that included the phrase "We are spirits in a material world." Sting may not have meant exactly the same thing as Paul, who wrote, "We brought nothing into the world, and we can take nothing out of it" (1 Timothy 6:7, NIV), but the idea is similar. We are more than seventy-some years of life-pumping heart, expanding lungs, and dividing cells. We are more than synapses, tendons, and an assortment of bladders. We have an eternal quality about us. If we serve money rather than making it a servant of God's kingdom, then we cast off the divine likeness we carry and take up an ultimately futile chase.

An old Jewish saying teaches: "A person is born naked with hands grasping, but there is nothing in them. When he leaves this life, his hands are folded over his chest, but there is still nothing in them." Likewise, the Christian who hopes in the promise of eternal life has the freedom to detach from material gain. Indeed, material life can be lived with eternal purpose, and money can be harnessed for service in God's kingdom. Why participate in a idolatrous pursuit of money when that pursuit contradicts the hope of Christianity?

Principle 3: Our use of money tells others about our worldview.

Each time we make a purchase, decide on an investment, or give a gift, we communicate what we care about. Checkbook ledgers and stacks of receipts reveal our most tightly held values. Therefore, our use of money communicates our worldview; a standard by

---

2. Burkholder, "Money: Master or Servant?" 783–84.

which reality is managed and pursued, a set of hinges on which all our everyday thinking and doing turns.[3]

Worldviews influence more than one's moral code or priorities. A worldview combines our experiences, our perceptions, and our convictions with our faith, ethics, physical capacity, and network of relationships to form our view of life. Worldviews are seldom clearly thought through or consistent, but they determine our actions.

Paul talks pretty plainly in his letter to Timothy. Notice Paul's conviction: that looking at a person's use of money reveals the heart. Jesus highlighted that truth, too, when he said, "Where your treasure is, there your heart will be also" (Matthew 6:21, NIV). Whether or not we talk openly about what is most important to us, how we use money gives us away.

Summary

Stewardship responsibilities sometimes get lumped into the three T's: Time (not wasting one's allotment of years), Talent (not wasting one's abilities), and Treasure (not wasting one's money), as if they were all equal. In fact, they are not. Unlike Time and Talent, Treasure has a godlike strength because we think it can make us happy. Treasure can dominate and twist the human spirit if not held in check by a more powerful master.

Reflections

What do the following uses of money reveal about the person's worldview?

    a. Jeff Lenacher's credit card debt equals two months of his salary. He pays 4 percent of each month's wages just to keep the balance from increasing. He pays an additional 5 percent of his monthly wages to try to bring the balance down. His continued use of credit for impulse purchases keeps the monthly

3. Bosch, *Believing in the Future*, 49.

balance from diminishing. He has considered closing his credit cards, but the rewards he gets from using the cards help him pick up little extras for the kids.

b. Both Liz Stone and Carolyn O'Brien live below the official poverty line. Liz hold down a job, accepts government assistance to supplement her grocery income, and lives in an extended family where everyone contributes to household expenses. Carolyn has been on the street since she was fifteen. No one taught her how to form a spending plan and she has no concept of saving for tomorrow. She uses whatever money she can scare up for liquor and an occasional meal.

c. Sebastian Dean is an entrepreneur who made hundreds of millions in the 1990s during the Internet boom. He saw the potential of the Internet before many major companies, so he purchased desirable domain names for cheap and sold them to companies at a premium rate. He lives very comfortably in a 15,000 square-foot newly renovated English Tudor. He collects vintage cars and owns several beachfront properties in Hawaii. In addition to these possessions, Mr. Dean intentionally seeks out ways to partner with organizations. He has paid for over 200 clean water wells to be drilled for people in Mozambique along with payment for over 200 new church structures to be built alongside each one. His work life now consists of investing in new start-ups in his home state to create new local jobs and to create new personal income. Next on his list to purchase is a '65 red Ford Mustang hardtop with only 852 original miles and next on his list to donate is a new state-of-the-art children's hospital in his city.

d. José Martinez owns a web design and hosting business with 73 employees. The business fills a needed niche in the industry, and he works hard to provide an atmosphere of friendship and team management, along with above-average wages. After another, larger, tech firm downsized last year in the next county over, his personnel office was flooded with résumés from people who desperately want to get on the payroll. The biggest customer José's company hosts, however, is a well-known adult content site.

e. Mary and Patrick Franz-Schlatter intentionally reduced their income to poverty level and homestead on a five-acre lot a few miles outside of town. Their reduced income means they no longer contribute taxes to the military-industrial complex. They also minimized their consumption of fossil fuel and use the land to produce much of what they need. By making this intentional move, they now contribute very little to the tax base of their community and had to cut their charitable contributions by 75 percent. At the same time, they have more time to give to community and world peace projects.

f. Benny Smith spends $25 a week, or $1,300 a year, on lottery tickets out of a $13,000 income. After two years his winnings total $650. He has implicit trust in the tic-tac-toe game, because more than half of his winnings came from playing it. Each week, he and his brother and his cousin get together over wings to discuss their results and their upcoming strategy for the next game. Each time he has won, Benny gave half to the community homeless shelter.

Suggestions

a. Compile a list of five of your most cherished values. Compare this to your family-spending plan. Make note of discrepancies between what you state is important and your use of money. Initiate steps to change your spending habits.

b. Lead a family brainstorming session about how you can live more generously. If you live alone, treat a close friend or two to dinner and ask them to help you brainstorm. (Hint: Treating a friend or two to dinner is a good start!)

c. Ask your small group or Sunday school class to help you identify a Christian worldview. Ask them to help you identify how money can serve this worldview instead of distort it.

d. Talk about your use of money more openly. Talk about your temptations. North Americans tend to treat money as a private issue. The problem is that secrecy about money gives additional power to something already godlike, and makes bad habits difficult to break alone. Your openness to discuss the struggle for an integrity between faith and finances begins to break destructive power and builds accountability for new and better choices.

3

God at Work

*Belief: Christians are called to share God's values—that is,
to view and respond to the world the way God does.*

THIS CHAPTER DETAILS BIBLICAL descriptions of God's work among us—from Eden, to Israel's covenant with God, to Isaiah's description of God's new society, to John's vision of the New Jerusalem. These descriptions demonstrate that the Christian's worldview is to be entwined with God's agenda to restore the universe. God's vision for the universe is revealed in Christ's work. Christians are called to share God's values—that is, to view and respond to creation the way God does.

The global Christian community agrees on the following:

a. God created the universe and it was good

b. Something happened that made our world less than perfect.

c. God, in Christ, plans to restore the universe to its intended purpose.

d. The way we live now ought to honor what God is doing.

Different Christian traditions might disagree over the method God used in creation, the means by which creation fell, just who Jesus Christ is, and what the restored universe will look like. But the heart of the Christian worldview is this: We believe our world is corrupted and hope that God, through Jesus Christ, is doing something to set things right.

The following Bible passages reveal God's view of the world, and thus provide guides for a Christian set of values.

Eden's Wealth (Genesis 1 and 2)

Read these familiar creation stories with the intent to identify the wealth and provision God built into creation. By doing so, we will discover what God wanted to give humanity:

a. A living system of light and darkness, water and dry land, heat and cool, male and female sexuality, all of which produce abundant vegetation and animal life (Genesis 1:1-25; 2:4-9)

b. An ability to join God in managing creation (Genesis 1:26-2:1; 2:15-20). Combine this with God's creation of humanity in the divine image (Genesis 1:26), and we see God giving humans a meaningful existence.

c. A rhythm of work and relaxation (Genesis 2:2-3).

d. Relationships and intimacy (Genesis 2:20-25).

e. Long, if not eternal, life (Genesis 2:9; 3:22).

f. An ability to choose God's way—to enter into a two-way relationship with the divine (Genesis 2:9; 15-17).

The creation stories leave the impression that God wanted an eternal arrangement with humanity. God built a world to provide an abundant supply for what humans need to live and to enjoy a close relationship with their Creator. The Genesis descriptions of Eden's paradise could be illustrated like this:

Eden's Wealth

Long Life
Moral Choice
Fellowship with God
Relationships/Intimacy
Meaningful Existence
Abundant Supply

1

Israel's Plenty (Deuteronomy 28)

Something broke in Eden. The two humans placed in this paradise exercised the gift of choice to seek a way other than God's. The result was a broken paradise. Humans still live longer than most plants and animals. They still have opportunity to know God and experience divine love. Humans still form relationships and experience intimacy. The earth still produces food. But it is not the same. Sin brought new realities of disease, death, and decay.

So God called out the Hebrew people to be the agents by which God could again bring all the good things intended for humanity. God rescued them from slavery, guided their way in the wilderness preserved them from their enemies, and saw to their basic needs. We are heirs to this rescue, to this care, to these promises, and thus *we* are also part of the story.

In this Exodus experience, God formed a relationship with the Hebrew people, and hence with all of us. Deuteronomy 28 tells of God's promises to the Hebrews, promises conditioned on their faithfulness to the covenant God wanted to make with them:

a. I will set you above all the nations of the earth. You will be the head, not the tail. You will be at the top, not at the bottom (vv. 1, 13).

---

1. Reprinted by permission from page 23, December 1989 issue of Sojourners, 2401 15th St. NW, Washington, DC 20009, 800 714-7474.

b. I will grant you a blessed life, both in urban and rural areas. Your children will be blessed. Your crops will be blessed. Your livestock will be blessed. Your food supply will be blessed. Your travel will be blessed. Your barns will be blessed. Your undertakings will be blessed (vv. 2-6, 8).

c. I will defeat your enemies (v. 7).

d. I will establish you as my holy people (v. 9).

e. I will make you abound in prosperity (v. 11).

f. I will grant you rain in its season (v. 12).

g. I will make you wealthy enough that you will be a lender to others, never a borrower (v. 12).

h. I will grant you opportunity to choose to live in these blessings by obeying my commands (v. 13).

The previous diagram of Eden's wealth can be expanded to include Israel's plenty. It may look like this:

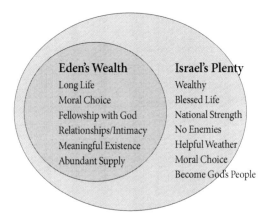

Eden's Wealth
Long Life
Moral Choice
Fellowship with God
Relationships/Intimacy
Meaningful Existence
Abundant Supply

Israel's Plenty
Wealthy
Blessed Life
National Strength
No Enemies
Helpful Weather
Moral Choice
Become God's People

2

---

2. From Inside the American Religious Scene, May 1990.

God's New Society (Isaiah 65:17-25)

This system also experienced periodic breakdown and repair. The Hebrews repeatedly abandoned their birthright for false gods and unrighteous living. At the end of the Old Testament era, the prophet Isaiah looks ahead to a new society that God will create. This new paradise is not a return to Eden's innocence. Rather, it includes God's deep-flowing grace to heal pain and *restore* the universe to its intended place. Isaiah describes God's new society as:

Happy (Isaiah 65:17-19)

- God commands eternal gladness and rejoicing in the new creation (v. 18).
- The people who live there are a joy to behold (v. 18).
- The newly created Jerusalem brings delight. Weeping and crying are removed (v. 19).

Healthy (Isaiah 65:20)

Infant mortality disappears. Citizen of the new society enjoy complete and expanded life expectancies. To dream of a society where children do not die, where disease is absent, and where righteousness is rewarded with long life, is to picture paradise.

Just (Isaiah 65:21,22)

God creates a society where land is fairly distributed, where people can live in homes they build, and in which nobody fills their bellies with crops forcibly taken from another. Justice—especially with land use—is a value God created within this new society.

Full of Dignity (Isaiah 65:22-24)

The society God intends to create also grants dignity to people. God says, "My chosen ones will long enjoy the works of their hands. They will not toil in vain or bear children doomed to misfortune; for they will be a people blessed by the Lord, they and their descendants with them. Before they call I will answer; while they are still speaking I will hear" (NIV).

- The society God creates provides fulfilling work for its people. There are no unfair labor practices. Nobody gets forced into jobs that destroy dignity.

- People shall not labor as slaves for another, with no hope for the well-being and dignity of their descendants.

- Those who try to seek God in this life often find communication hindered, but in God's new society all hindrances are removed.

Peaceful (Isaiah 65:25)

Natural enemies within the animal kingdom become the best of friends. Carnivores become herbivores. Dangerous serpents become as harmless as house pets. God's new society is peaceful.

With the expanded view of Isaiah's description we add a new layer to a description of paradise. [3]

The New Jerusalem (Revelation 21:1-22:5)

Between Isaiah's vision and John's vision of the future comes the advent of Jesus, the Messiah, and the beginning of the church. At Jesus' birth, Mary, Simeon, Zechariah, and the angels all sang about God doing something new in the coming of Jesus. In the midst of this "new thing," despotic rulers find their thrones upside down. Oppressed people gain new freedom. Poor people find access to

3. Schlabach, *And Who is My Neighbor?*, 50.

wealth. Most important, those who join God's community would be able to practice their faith in freedom (Luke 1:73-75).

Clearly Isaiah's vision of God's new society enlivened the New Testament Christians, but as we discover in John's vision of heaven, the understanding of paradise expands yet again.

a. The Old Testament vision of God's new society was of people building homes and being able to live in them without fear of their being taken away. The New Testament vision is of Jesus himself preparing the place where we will live.

b. The Old Testament vision is of extended life, and death only when sin is present. The New Testament vision is of eternal life and the total absence of sin.

c. The Old Testament vision is of eating the fruit of one's labor. The New Testament is one of abundant provision.

d. The Old Testament vision is of the nearness of God's aid. The New Testament promises a heaven where God actually pitches a tent among humanity and lives with us.

e. The Old Testament teaches us to appreciate the new society God creates. The New Testament gives us God's new address— planet earth

The language of Revelation 21 and 22 is symbolic. Several opinions exist about each symbol's meaning. Yet the gist of this passage is clear: there will be a new heaven and a new earth, and God will live with us in the New Jerusalem John describes the New Jerusalem as follows.

God will bring a new order to creation (Revelation 21:1-5)

The problems with the old heaven and the old earth disappear. What humans destroyed in pride and ignorance God now restores. This New Jerusalem comes down out of heaven, and is God's capital, God's dwelling. The New Jerusalem has no more death or mourning or crying or pain. Laughter is heard where once crying was the only sound. Pain is replaced by well-being. When God comes to live with us, the neighborhood property values go up!

God's dwelling will have high standards
(Revelation 21:6-8, 27)

This does not mean God hosts an exclusive party. Instead, the admission ticket to God's dwelling is for anyone thirsty enough to overcome. The *first standard* for entering God's dwelling is desire. Anyone who really wants to can get in. But the *second standard*, overcoming obstacles to faith, must also be met. Overcoming means getting past the obstacles or hindrances to faith in order to drink of the water of life. Just musing over what it would be like to thirst after God is not enough. One must actually do it. There is an important difference! What must one overcome? According to John, examples include personal fears, detestable actions, murder or sexual immorality without repentance, the practice of magic arts, idolatry, and deceit.

Surely God's standards are high, but God does not require people to quench their thirst before entering the kingdom. He requires only that they sincerely thirst for the water only God can give, and that they start drinking.

God's dwelling will be in the Holy City
(Revelation 21:9- 26)

First, the New Jerusalem will unite heaven and earth. Our eternal dwelling is an earthly city, built in heaven, and resting on this planet. In Christ, we can reach out to God in our prayers and God responds to us. But in the New Jerusalem, our access to God will be much closer and better. God becomes our neighbor!

Second, the New Jerusalem symbolizes God's perfection. Note how the measurements of the New Jerusalem describe a perfect cube, just like the holy of holies in Solomon's temple (1 Kings

6:20). No longer is God's glory confined to a small sanctuary the priest enters just once a year, curtained off from human eyes. God's glory now fills a city, vast and perfect in size.

Third, the New Jerusalem reflects God's abundance. It is not a false abundance like we experience in North America—abundance that means austere existence for someone else. God's mere presence produces fitting and abundant surroundings. This great wealth reflects the glory of New Jerusalem's First Citizen.

Last, the New Jerusalem provides light to the nations. Another way of saying this is that God's dwelling becomes the center of God's government. No longer will this world labor under self-serving governments. Instead, earth's kings lead the way in service to God!

God's dwelling brings an eternal identity (Revelation 22:1-5)

In the New Jerusalem all question about spiritual identity ceases. All doubts about salvation disappear. God marks the foreheads of heaven's citizens, and they shall no longer fear the face of the divine.

A final layer can now be added to the biblical picture of paradise:[4]

---

4. Koontz, *Godward: Personal Stories of Grace*, 56.

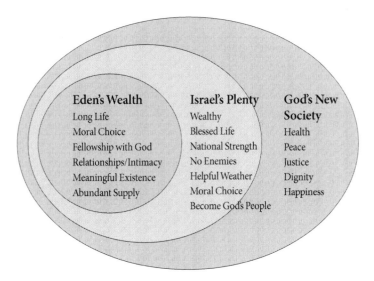

Eden's Wealth
Long Life
Moral Choice
Fellowship with God
Relationships/Intimacy
Meaningful Existence
Abundant Supply

Israel's Plenty
Wealthy
Blessed Life
National Strength
No Enemies
Helpful Weather
Moral Choice
Become God's People

God's New
Society
Health
Peace
Justice
Dignity
Happiness

Summary

In the story of Eden, in God's covenant with Israel, in Isaiah's vision of God's new society, and in John's description of the New Jerusalem, we find an expanding understanding of what God wants to provide all humanity. God's vision for the universe is revealed in Christ's work, and is meant to be the basis of the Christian worldview.

In the next chapter we explore how this worldview influences the Christian's use of money.

Reflections

What do the following uses of money reveal about the person's worldview?

a. Samuel Washington stands on a street corner every Friday and Saturday evening at the busiest intersection of a major metropolis. Each weekend he proclaims the same biblical text: "As it is written in the book of the words of the prophet

Isaiah, 'The voice of one crying out in the wilderness: "Prepare the way of the Lord, make his paths straight. Every valley shall be filled, and every mountain and hill shall be made low, and the crooked shall be made straight, and the rough ways made smooth; and all flesh shall see the salvation of God"'" (Luke 3:4-6, NRSV). Anyone who stays to listen is invited to a local church for Sunday services.

b. David and Blossom Chan, a married couple, joined a Franciscan lay community in order to devote themselves to prayer and service to God. Although they don't always enjoy living in such an intentional community, they certainly prefer it to the high-pressure professional jobs they once held.

c. The Posterski family pools the income from wife and husband to live in a larger-than-average home in a better-than-average neighborhood. They also drive larger-than-average vehicles that get worse-than-average gas mileage. They regularly donate their vehicles for use in church and community functions, and often donate the gasoline. They also try to host two dinner parties a month in their home according to the principles of James 2:1-7.

d. Beth Ann Danforth reads a lot of books on biblical prophecy and how these prophecies are coming true today. Although she does not think it is appropriate to predict a date for Christ's return, she does think it will be soon. "Besides," Beth says, "if Jesus doesn't return in my lifetime, it doesn't matter. I'm supposed to live ready to go at any time-always watching the skies for the glory of God, and always listening for that last trumpet."

e. Emily Lennox was delighted when her daughter, Kaitlynn, was chosen to be on the sixth-grade traveling soccer club team. Kaitlynn shows so much potential— she's good at volleyball and track, too. Games are typically held on Sundays, so Emily and Kaitlynn aren't getting to church as often. Since she's a single mom, and she wants to stay involved with Kaitlynn's life, Emily travels with the team as a chaperone. The costs of the uniforms, meals out, souvenirs, and incidentals stretch the family budget. Emily makes sure, though, to cover the dinner cost of at least one other girl on the team each week whose family sends her with a sack lunch, so she doesn't feel left out. Emily set up an automatic online payment to her church so she can continue to give while they're away—which is about three weekends per month.

Suggestions

a. Review your understanding of heaven and God's purpose in offering it to us. How does your understanding compare to the descriptions provided in this chapter?

b. Before reading the next chapter, identify how you think the Christian's worldview should influence your use of money.

c. Plan a worship service with your small group or congregation around the Bible passages explored in this chapter. Use hymns that celebrate creation, that retell God's covenant with Israel, that rejoice in God's new society, and that look forward to God living with us in the New Jerusalem.

d. Spend time with other passages that point to God's intentions for the universe. List what you find and compare it to the material in this chapter. See if you can identify additional ingredients found in God's restored universe. See Isaiah 55; Ezekiel 47:1-12; Matthew 25; 1 Thessalonians 4:14—5:11; 2 Peter 3:1 - 13.

e. Reflect on how people in your community (your friends, family, and church family) define wealth. Compare it to the wealth found in the biblical vision of what God wants to provide. What similarities or differences do you discover?

4

Kingdom Citizens

Belief: Because of our citizenship in God's kingdom and our loyalty to God's values, our joyful response is to give our life's work to God's service, and to use wealth in cooperation with God's values.

THE PREVIOUS CHAPTER (3) detailed biblical descriptions of God's work among us—from Eden, to Israel's covenant with God, to Isaiah's description of God's new society, to John's vision of the New Jerusalem. These descriptions show that the Christian's worldview is to be entwined with God's agenda to restore the universe. This chapter moves us toward the natural result of the Christian's worldview, especially in the use of money. If we want to be identified with God's work as described in the Bible then we must value what God values, and expend our energy the way God would. Christians are extensions of God's personality to a broken world.

> "So if anyone is in Christ, there is a new creation: everything old has passed away; see, everything has become new! All this is from God, who reconciled us to himself through Christ, and has given us the ministry of reconciliation; that is, in Christ God was reconciling the world to himself, not counting their trespasses against them, and entrusting the message of reconciliation to us. So we are ambassadors for Christ, since God is making his appeal through us; we entreat you on behalf of Christ, be reconciled to God" (2 Corinthians 5:17-20, NRSV).

While Christians wait for the Lord's return and the final establishment of God's kingdom, they set aside a human point of view and become God's agents of reconciliation. They become God's representatives, and model God's character. To be Christian—to identify with God's purposes—is to look at the world as God sees it, and to use one's life to further God's work. The following passages describe God's caring, work, and purpose.

The Bible has many pleas for God's people to take on the character of God:

> "Be holy because I, the Lord your God, am holy" (Leviticus 19:2, NIV)

> "Be perfect, therefore, as your heavenly Father is perfect" (Matthew 548, NIV).

> "Be imitators of God, therefore, as dearly loved children and live a life of love, just as Christ loved us and gave himself up for us as a fragrant offering and sacrifice to God" (Ephesians 5:1, NIV)

> "We do not want you to become lazy, but to imitate those who through faith and patience inherit what has been promised" (Hebrews 6:12, NIV)

> "Has not God chosen those who are poor in the eyes of the world to be rich in faith and to inherit the kingdom he promised those who love him? But you have insulted the poor" (James 2:5-6, NIV).

> "Whoever says, 'I abide in him,' ought to walk just as. [Jesus] walked" (1 John 2:6, NRSV)

> "Dear friend, do not imitate what is evil but what is good. Anyone who does what is good is from God. Anyone who does what is evil has not seen God" (3 John 11, NIV).

God's extravagant love and grace (Titus 3:3-8)

The letter to Titus provides one of the most profound descriptions of this great love:

"At one time we too were foolish, disobedient, deceived and enslaved by all kinds of passions and pleasures. We lived in malice and envy, being hated and hating one another. But when the kindness and love of God our Savior appeared, he saved us, not because of righteous things we had done, but because of his mercy. He saved us through the washing of rebirth and renewal by the Holy Spirit, whom he poured out on us generously through Jesus Christ our Savior, so that, having been justified by his grace, we might become heirs having the hope of eternal life. This is a trustworthy saying. And I want you to stress these things, so that those who have trusted in God may be careful to devote themselves to doing what is good. These things are excellent and profitable for everyone" (Titus 3:3-8, NIV).

To be Christian is to identify with God's purposes- is to look at the world as God sees it. to take on God's character, and to use one's life to further God's work.

We desperately need God (v. 3).

Sin is a problem for all humans. We are not worms. Nor are we angels. We are like angels with a bad case of worms. In spite of the goodness God created in us, we become disobedient, deceptive, slaves to passion, and are violent. God wants us to acknowledge our part in the corruption and to move to a greater godliness. Our hope for healing rests in our Creator.

God 's kindness and love brings salvation, not human effort (vv. 4-7)

All the righteous works we attempt cannot provide the rescue from our misery. God's mercy alone is the agent of salvation. Paul's words seem to drip with God's great kindness. God saved us. God washed us. God rebirthed and renewed us. God poured out the

Holy Spirit on us. God was generous with us. God gives us an inheritance. God gives us a hope of eternal life.

> Our family once shared our home with Mariah. a border collie mutt. When she dug her first hole in the flower bed, it dyed her snow-white front legs a rich chocolate. When I called her in from outside, she came bounding up the back porch totally unaware she was about to track earth on our carpets. She had no knowledge of her dirty condition. It was all great fun to her.
>
> We always kept a throw rug by the back door. And taught our dogs to sit and have their paws wiped whenever they come in. When I saw Mariah coming, it was clear no paw wiping would work this time. I scooped her up and took her straight to the tub for a bath. She didn't like the bath very much, and giving her one was not high on my list of priorities either. But I love dogs, and I was more than willing to put up with the messes and headaches for the special companionship and fun my family received in return.
>
> God's treatment of us is similar. We may not fully understand how needy we are, yet God remains ready to scoop us up, bathe us, anoint us, and give us a place in a heavenly home God seems more than willing to put up with the messes and headaches for a chance at companionship with humans who choose to respond to this great tenderness.

God's extravagant love molds the Christian worldview (v. 8)

Because God's kindness, cleansing, anointing, and inheritance met us in our broken and needy state, Christians continue God's tradition of mercy. The connection to money comes here. Because we take on God's character of extravagant mercy we harness money's power for that purpose. We support efforts to share God's extravagant love with other needy and broken people.

God shares the earth's blessings with all inhabitants (Luke 6:27-35; Matthew 5:45)

Our planet holds an abundant supply of water. The sun shines brightly. The earth is layered with topsoil and natural fertilizers. God doesn't grant these blessings to Christians only. All humans benefit from them. Our lives depend on this light, water, good soil, and warmth, far more than on lucrative job promotions, a larger house, or a child who cooperates with the rest of the household.

Jesus adds an interesting twist to this understanding:

> "But I tell you who hear me: Love your enemies, do good to those who hate you, bless those who curse you, pray for those who mistreat you. If someone strikes you on one cheek, turn to him the other also. If someone takes your cloak, do not stop him from taking your tunic. Give to everyone who asks you, and if anyone takes what belongs to you, do not demand it back. Do to others as you would have them do to you.
>
> "If you love those who love you, what credit is that to you? Even 'sinners' love those who love them. And if you do good to those who are good to you, what credit is that to you? Even 'sinners' do that. And if you lend to those from whom you expect repayment, what credit is that to you? Even 'sinners' lend to 'sinners,' expecting to be repaid in full. But love your enemies, do good to them, and lend to them without expecting to get anything back. Then your reward will be great, and you will be sons of the Most High, because he is kind to the ungrateful and wicked' (Luke 6:27-35, NIV).

In Matthew's version, the teaching is even clearer:

> "[The Father] causes his sun to rise on the evil and the good, and sends rain on the righteous and the unrighteous" (Matthew 5:45, NIV).

Jesus teaches that those who follow God are motivated to love like God does. God shows kindness even to ungrateful and wicked people. God's mercy shows up in well-distributed sunshine and rain. Christians, who understand God's kindness and mercy, will scatter their love just as generously. Sharing God's merciful love with all people is to be their distinction.

Ask yourself this question: If this story were moved to the twentieth century, what part would North Americans play? Would they be Jesus? The disciples? The oppressor? To many Christians in other countries, North American society represents the enemy Jesus commands disciples to bless, the abuser for whom they must turn the other cheek, the greedy consumer to whom they contribute upon demand, the other to whom they do good amid the growing impossibility of its being returned. They love North Americans because God gives us sunshine and rain, too

What would it mean for North American Christians, truly committed to God's agenda, to start loving the world in this way? For one thing, North American dollars would be used to distribute more fairly this earth's resources among the world's population. North American people committed to God's kingdom would also begin thinking globally, because they know God is preparing a people from all languages and nations. This does not mean that North American Christians have to grasp all the nuances of international politics. Instead, their global view may be as simple as sending money through a relief organization to improve the quality of life for someone in need.

> A checklist for deciding which evangelistic efforts to support or participate in:
>
> a. Does the ministry call people into the kingdom in the same spirit God used in calling us?
>
> b. Does it invite people to be washed, rebirthed. renewed, and anointed?
>
> c. Does it call people into a hope and inheritance?
>
> If so, we can joyfully participate. If not, there is good reason to believe God's character is not well represented.

They might also adjust shopping habits to support organizations committed to supplying artisans and laborers with a fair wage. North American Christians committed to sharing the earth's resources would also move toward a detachment from personal possessions, letting believers in the other two-thirds of the world call them toward a growing spiritual maturity and material simplicity.

In the book *Habits of the Heart*, a woman named Nan, a long way from her Christian upbringing, retains at least this much wisdom about the Christian faith and God's view of the world: "We're all on this earth. Just because I was fortunate to be born in America and white doesn't make me any better than someone that's born in Africa and is black. They deserve to eat just as much as I deserve to eat. The boat people have the same feelings that I do. The same feelings- how can we say no to them?"[1]

God brings shalom/aloha/salaam

Shalom, aloha, and salaam are all encompassing words used to say hello, good-bye, best wishes, peace, harmony, wholeness, and sufficiency. God promised the spirit of these words, a spirit growing from living strong in God's grace. Our relationship with God is restored. We find new purpose in our existence. The money we manage in God's behalf becomes an instrument of bringing this well-being to others.

Consider God's instruction to protect the weak, both in the Old Testament and the New (all quotes are from the NRSV):

Old Testament

"When you buy a male Hebrew slave, he shall serve six years, but in the seventh he shall go out a free person, without debt" (Exodus 21:2).

"If you lend money to my people, to the poor among you, you shall not deal with them as a creditor; you shall not exact interest from them" (Exodus 22:25).

---

1. Bellah, et al., *Habits of the Heart*, 229.

"You shall not oppress a resident alien; you know the heart of an alien, for you were aliens in the land of Egypt" (Exodus 23:9).

"For six years you shall sow your land and gather in its yield; but the seventh year you shall let it rest and lie fallow, so that the poor of your people may eat; and what they leave the wild animals may eat. You shall do the same with your vineyard, and with your olive orchard" (Exodus 23: 10).

"Every seventh year you shall grant a remission of debts" (Deuteronomy 15:1).

"If there is among you anyone in need, a member of your community in any of your towns within the land that the Lord your God is giving you, do not be hard-hearted or tight-fisted toward your needy neighbor. You should rather open your hand, willingly lending enough to meet the need, whatever it may be" (Deuteronomy 15:7-8).

"You shall not deprive a resident alien or an orphan of justice; you shall not take a widow's garment in pledge. Remember that you were a slave in Egypt and the Lord your God redeemed you from there . . . " (Deuteronomy 24:17-18) .

"When an alien resides with you in your land, you shall not oppress the alien. The alien who resides with you shall be to you as the citizen among you; you shall love the alien as yourself, for you were aliens in the land of Egypt: I am the Lord your God" (Leviticus 19:33, 34).

New Testament

From Matthew 25:34-35 . . .

"The king will say to those at his right hand, 'Come, you that are blessed by my Father, inherit the kingdom prepared for you from the foundation of the world; for I was hungry and you gave me food, I was a stranger and you welcomed me, I was thirsty and you gave me something to drink, I was naked and you gave me clothing,

From James 1:27 . . .

"Religion that is pure and undefiled before God, the Father, is this: to care for orphans and widows in their distress, and to keep oneself unstained by the world.

Summary

Christian people, citizens of God's kingdom, are to be loyal to kingdom values. These values are part of God's personality and should be qualities found in God's children.

These values include God's extravagant love and grace to broken people, God's sharing of this earth's blessings with all who inhabit it, and the spirit of Shalom/aloha/salaam. Therefore, the Christian's joyful response means using money as an instrument of Shalom/aloha/salaam. Christians who think globally share God's concern for the poor, and they proclaim the good news of salvation in Jesus Christ.

Reflections

Based on the material of this chapter, what counsel would you give to the following people?

a. David Jackson consistently overeats. His waistline expanded through three wardrobes in five years. Each time David out-girthed the contents of his closet, he gave the best of those clothes to a clothing distribution ministry. David got a nice tax deduction for the gift.

b. JoAnne Modlin has a call to preach. The entire church community affirms this special gift. JoAnne is considering using this gift in an evangelistic ministry and wonders if the congregation would provide financial support. She is pledged to thorough accountability. But some congregational members question whether the style of evangelism is appropriate.

c. The Paluzzi family is building a house on the outskirts of town on a wooded waterfront lot. They reduced the cost by doing much of the interior work themselves, and they are using the money saved to make a substantial contribution to Mrs. Paluzzi's alma mater's minority scholarship fund. The Paluzzis tell everyone they are moving from their urban environment because they always wanted more of a country place, but this is little more than a smoke screen for the real reason. The Paluzzis decided to build now because a minority ethnic group was starting to move into the neighborhood, and they were worried about property values.

d. Herman Belmann has an opportunity to invest in a Bolivian peasant's entrepreneurial dream, or to give directly to a needy family through a relief organization. His financial situation does not allow him to do both.

e. Jim and Leona Dunkirk, a Christian married couple, live next door to a single mother of three. The children are often in the street until well after dark, unsupervised and dirty. The ages of the children roughly correspond to Jim and Leona's offspring. The previous week the single mother approached Leona and wondered about forming a play group with the children from both families. Leona asked for some time to think about it.

f. LaTosha Poinsatte is an airline executive whose company has a long history of providing free seats for needy people. LaTosha is currently overseeing a $2 Billion first-class cabin renovation project on all domestic and international flights. Her airline does not want to lose its market share in the luxury class, so they are making more leg room, providing continuous snack service, and keeping the world's best wines at hand for those willing to pay a premium. Meanwhile, the economy-class seats are getting closer together and they have cut all meal service on domestic flights under six hours. LaTosha says her airline must keep attracting wealthy people so that profit margins remain high enough to let them keep giving free seats for medical emergencies, refugee resettlement, and the Make-A-Wish Foundation.

Suggestions

a. Answer these questions: Is your worldview connected to a profound experience of God's grace? Does your Christian worldview express itself in your words, your choices, your responses in relationships? Or has your Christian commitment become separated and hidden so as not to intrude on others?

b. Identify one additional way you will reduce, reuse, or recycle as a means to live a less consumptive lifestyle.

c. Choose a lesser developed country about which you would like to know more. Go to the library and read about its history, commerce, and people. Take special note of its per capita income, and just what that income can purchase. Compare it to your earnings and lifestyle. Then, instead of thanking God for letting you live in North America so you can have more, consider how you can joyfully celebrate God's abundant provision with a person from this other nation.

d. Reflect on why we tend to separate the gospel message from relief and service work. Why do we think we must choose between pounding nails and testifying verbally to our faith? How can you better integrate the two in your understanding of what God intends to do?

e. Try to invest in companies or programs that emphasize development and a better quality of life over those who make weapons, treat their workers unfairly in order to maximize profits, or whose products promote addictions.

f. Start forming long-term relationships with people in your community who have long-term need. Connect personally with someone who is mentally ill. Give blood. Join the PTA at an at-risk school. Visit an imprisoned relative. Dream up something new.

5

Creator, Provider, Redeemer, King, and Cause

Belief: As we live our beliefs about money, we must remember that God accomplishes saving work through Jesus, the Christ and Lord of the universe.

WHEN YOU HEAR THE name of Jesus, what picture comes to mind? Do you see the baby in Bethlehem honored by angels, shepherds, and magi? Do you picture the intelligent child who challenged learned rabbis in theological conversation? Do you think of the radical Preacher who proclaimed the nearness of God's kingdom and invited repentance? Do you picture the great Teacher who held the attention of thousands without a public address system, and invited them to the ethics of the Sermon on the Mount? Do you remember the Miracle Worker-healing lepers, feeding hungry people, restoring life, commanding demons, and calming storms? Do you recall the donkey-riding King who received the praises of crowds of people on Palm Sunday? Do you see the crucified Savior? Do you picture an empty tomb, a resurrected Jesus who invited Thomas to touch his wounds? Do you see a risen Savior ascending into heaven to prepare a place for us?

Mistakes of Holding an Incomplete View of Jesus

Lack of real purpose

Jesus as a baby stirs up affection, but it does not save or grant entrance to heaven. Jesus as a great Teacher may help us make friends and influence people, but it grants us no eternal destination. Jesus as Savior might rescue us from sin, but it leaves us unclear about what we are saved to do, and just what it is we offer to others. Understanding the person and work of Jesus-our Creator, our Provider, our Redeemer, our King, and our Cause gives us a deeper grounding and a greater purpose.

Mere reciprocal giving

An incomplete view of Jesus can also leave us with weak motivation for a lifetime of generosity. If Jesus is only the Bethlehem baby, our giving comes from sentiment. Where we feel no sentiment, we give no gift. If Jesus is only a Teacher, we give to get a good grade—and only when we enjoy the subject! If Jesus is only a Savior, we end up giving to even the score, not because we have a grace motivation. Even reciprocal giving gets mired in law, obligation, and duty.

. . .

Reciprocal = responding in kind to something previously done for you by someone else.

. . .

When reciprocal giving arises from obligation, we lose touch with our need. Awareness of our own need prevents us from rationalizing why sin might be right, or from judging someone else's sin as more severe. Awareness of our own need for grace makes us better able to hold the hands of other sinners, and lead them into the kingdom. Awareness of our own need will make us more receptive to the leading of the Holy Spirit, who can also impress upon us the magnitude of the person and work of Jesus.

Loss of mission for the church

Yet another danger of an incomplete view of Jesus is what it means for the mission of the church. If Jesus is only an infant in a manger, the church gathers merely to pass on tradition and sentimental feelings. If Jesus is only a Teacher, the church exists as an educational institution to pass on a fixed body of doctrine. If Jesus is Savior only, then preaching the gospel and giving invitations to faith become the measure of success. The church with a proclaiming mission only has solely to talk to the lost. They have no reason to become ministers of mercy.

Sentimental traditions, doctrinal teaching, or even gospel preaching are not a sufficient mission for God's people. These missions do not require the church to extend the kingdom. Even the mission of proclamation makes no such requirement because all that matters is the preaching. Beam out the radio broadcasts and retreat behind the church walls!

The full picture

If, however, we meet Jesus as Creator, Provider, Redeemer, King, and Cause for our life, we know what it means to share in adoration of a Lamb who bought a people from every tribe, language, people, and nation (Revelation 5:9). If we accept what God, in Christ, intends to generously provide, we are rescued out of the kingdom of darkness into the kingdom of light. If we experience the vast chasm between our good intentions and our hopeless inadequacy, we are blessed because we know our need for God. When God's grace meets us, we realize that salvation means peace and wholeness, and we cannot hoard anything. We cannot be selfish with income or possessions because of the generous God we serve.

The great commission at the end of Matthew's gospel reminds us of the real mission: "Therefore go and make disciples of all nations, baptizing them in the name of the Father and of the Son and of the Holy Spirit" (Matthew 28:19 NIV).

Making disciples is our mission, not just getting them wet with baptismal waters! Making disciples requires living with those we seek to reach, having compassion for them, washing their feet, and understanding the depth of their need. The only motivation strong enough to sustain this mission is a relationship with Jesus as Creator, Provider, Redeemer, King, and Cause for our life. If Jesus is not everything to us, then we have insufficient resources to advance the mission of Christ's kingdom. When Christians truly embrace Jesus as Christ and Lord of the universe, including themselves, their use of money will reflect this gift of redemption and abundant life.

Summary

Jesus is Creator and Sustainer of the universe. He is gathering a kingdom of people unhindered by language or geography who will function as priests for the world. Jesus is worthy of all power, wealth, wisdom, strength, honor, glory, and praise. Jesus is where we meet God's generosity. Jesus oversees God's project of redeeming the world. Christians who fully acknowledge the person and work of Jesus are more likely to be transformed by God's abundant life and find a lifelong motivation for generous living.

Reflections

Based on information in this chapter, what counsel or admonishment would you give the following people?

a. The Evans family lives in a middle-class suburban neighborhood. Their property includes a privacy fence and backyard grill. They just installed a $10,000 security system to protect their collection of first-edition wildlife paintings. They like singing the hymn "Lift High the Cross" (321, Hymnal: A Worship Book).

Lift high the cross, the love of Christ proclaim

till all the world adore his sacred name.

O Lord, once lifted on the tree of pain,

draw all the world to seek you once again.

From north and south, from east and west, we raise

in growing unison our song of praise.

Let every race and every language tell

of him who saves our lives from death and hell.

Set up your throne, that earth's despair may cease

beneath the shadow of its healing peace.

—George W Kitchin, 1887[1]

Revised by Michael R. Newbolt, 1916

© 1974 Hope Publishing Co., Carol Stream, IL 60188.
All rights reserved. Used by permission.

They like the hymn so much that they have a collection of various recording artists performing it, and play it through their state-of-the-art sound systems in their twin Acura SUVs. Both SUVs also have security systems.

b. Jen Balzer, a Bible college graduate, had hoped to prepare for a missionary career. She needed to pay off her college debt, however, before any mission agency would send her. While working to pay off her debt, she fell in love and married someone who did not share her missionary zeal. Now Jen is a stay-at-home mother of three elementary school children, a Sunday school teacher, and an active participant in her congregation's missions committee. Still, somewhere deep inside, Jen grieves over the loss of some of her life options.

---

1. *Revised by Michael R. Newbolt, 1916* © 1974 Hope Publishing Co., Carol Stream, IL 60188. All rights reserved. Used by permission.

c. Adam Jacobssen accepted Jesus as his Savior at age eight. He was at Vacation Bible School and raised his hand when the invitation was given during the Sunday night closing worship service. Adam wasn't afraid of hell or anything like that. He just knew Jesus loved him. So did his family and the church he attended. It seemed a natural response then. Now at age 23, and living alone in a much larger city, Adam wonders if God is with him.

d. Tawnee and Darnelle Crascall were married three years ago and quickly outgrew apartment living. They began saving almost immediately for a house and are getting close to their 10 percent down-payment goal. Tawnee recently figured that if they cut financial contributions to their congregation by half, stop getting the local paper, and reduce their eating out by one meal a week, the money saved would be enough for the down payment a year from now. Then they can buy a house much closer to their church than their current thirty-minute commute, and they could be more involved in congregational life.

e. Samantha McAfree, a single mother, is a deeply committed Christian. Her economic survival depends on child support and her half-time job at a small florist shop for $2 per hour more than the minimum wage. She is the only employee. It is Valentine's Day season and they are buried in orders. A regular customer, whom the owner refers to as a "meal ticket," comes in to place an order for two dozen roses— one for his wife, the other for his girlfriend. Samantha doesn't care for this man's casual approach to morality, but she knows he accounts for 25 percent of the florist's business. Samantha works nearby as the owner fills the man's order. She notices that he accidentally put his wife's card in the mistress' envelope, and vice versa. At first she thinks it serves the man right to be found out. Then she wonders if the man will blame the florist for the mix-up and take his business elsewhere. This could mean her job. Yet, calling attention to his mistake would make her feel like she is helping him carry out his deception.

Suggestions

a. In a circle of friends, discuss your view of Jesus. How has it developed? What is your viewpoint now? Is there any connection between your understanding of Jesus and whatever generosity you show?

b. On a sheet of paper make two columns. On the left side list ways you currently serve as a priest to the world-both in close and distant places. On the right side, list additional steps you are willing to take. For more information of priestly functions, look at the following passages: Exodus 19 (v. 6 especially) ; Exodus 20:1-37; Hebrews 4:14-5:10; 1 Peter 2:9-10; Revelation 5 (especially v. 10).

c. If this chapter led you to a deeper relationship with Jesus the Messiah, plan to share publicly that new adoration in a congregational setting. You might even consider reaffirming your baptismal vows.

d. Imagine that someone develops a personality based on gift giving. Factors include the number of gifts given, the spirit in which they were given, the thoughtfulness behind the gift, the proportion of income used, and the expectations with which the gift was given. What would this test say about you?

e. If your congregation has a mission statement, evaluate it in light of the person and work of Jesus as described in this chapter. If your congregation does not have a mission statement, reflect on what you think most people from your church consider it to be. Does the statement reflect a limited or expanded understanding of Jesus?

6

Whole Life Dedication

Belief: When we joyfully meet God's grace in Jesus, we are empowered to live out our belief that God is Owner of all. We dedicate all of life in an act of worship to God. We commit ourselves to participate in God's saving work.

Scene 1: Jerusalem, first century

The church selected seven deacons to lead in their mercy ministries. The most noteworthy was Stephen known to be a man full of faith and the Holy Spirit. His notoriety led to a series of public disputes, but Stephen's Spirit-led teaching could not be successfully contested.

The leaders who could not beat Stephen in public debate sought a more underhanded way to silence him. They had Stephen arrested on trumped-up charges and brought before the Jewish ruling council. Stephen could defend himself, water down his interest in Jesus, and demonstrate his loyalty to the Jewish faith. Or he could publicly declare his undying loyalty to Jesus and his commitment to kingdom service at the risk of his life. There was no middle ground.

Scene 2: Rome, A.D. 303

During Emperor Maximian's persecution of the Christians, Victor, a French Christian, was noted for his generous work among the poor and sick. Maximian ordered Victor's arrest, at which time he was bound and dragged through the streets. While Victor's torture included getting stretched on the rack, the only change of heart was in his jailers. Maximian ordered the execution of Victor's jailers and renewed his torture of Victor. A small altar was brought to the chamber for Victor to offer incense and recognize the emperor as a deity. Maximian stood by to watch. All Victor had to do was put the pinch of incense on the altar and say Caesar is lord and his life would be spared.[1]

Scene 3: Austria, A.D. 1529

Those who opposed the Anabaptist movement arrested Christine Tollinger. She was taken to the castle of En for trial. Anabaptists did not believe in a state church, but in the sole government of God. Thus they were considered dangerous heretics. Her interrogators did not ask her to forsake belief in Jesus as the Christ. They wanted her merely to renounce her Anabaptist convictions.[2]

Scene 4: Bulgaria, A.D. 1948

Haralan Popov, a Bulgarian pastor, was imprisoned for more than thirteen years. He was beaten regularly, fed a scant "death diet," and forced to stand without sleep facing a bright white wall for two weeks. His persecutors wanted him to confess to espionage against the government. All he had to do was say he did it and the extreme torture would end.[3]

Each of these scenes holds something in common following Jesus meant declaring one's life, one's assets, one's family, and one's talents as holy unto God. There was no partial entrance into the kingdom. Stephen confronted the ruling council with his faith and became the first martyr of the early church. Victor

1. Forbush, ed., *Fox's Book of Martyrs*, 26.
2. *The Chronicle of the Hutterian Brethren*, 717.
3. Popov, *Tortured for His Faith*, 190.

kicked the altar over and was thrown into a mill and crushed. Christine Tollinger was executed for reaffirming her Anabaptist convictions. Haralan Popov resisted as long as he could, until he finally confessed to a crime he didn't commit. The modern brainwashing techniques Haralan experienced were not merciful like being stoned or getting crushed in a mill! Haralan served his thirteen years in Bulgarian concentration camps and returned to the pastorate after his release.

In the first century dedication was connected to conversion. When converts told God they were sorry for their sins and invited Jesus to be their Savior, they implicitly aligned themselves politically, socially, psychologically, emotionally, and physically with God's agenda to bring healing to the world. Middle ground did not exist. Were the Christians who faced persecution all spiritually mature before they were acceptable to God? Absolutely not! But they were clear on this: following Jesus meant not following other things.

Each scene presented a clear and drastic choice for the believer. Life belongs to the tyrant or to Christ's kingdom. These people had no opportunity to flirt with both as our North American society allows us. North American citizens are unique in that we rarely experience overt pressure to make a clear and drastic choice for Christ. Because our lives are not usually at risk when we publicly confess our faith, many of us merely give mental assent when we take our baptismal vows. Our risk-free Christianity allows us to join because we like a particular church in a particular moment, rather than making a pledge to a dedicated life. The result is many believers who have a Savior, but who do not yet honor Jesus as Lord.

Our wealthy society confuses us. We tend to think multiple pursuits and multiple loyalties are acceptable. But Jesus intended for us to understand a whole life dedication when he said, "Everyone who has left houses or brothers or sisters or father or mother or children or fields for my sake will receive a hundred times as much and will inherit eternal life" (Matthew I 9:29, NIV). Becoming Christian requires our pledge to dedicate all of our life to Jesus.

Christians must move off a comfortable salvation and into a whole life dedication.

The apostle James sent a stinging rebuke to Christians who separated their faith from whole life dedication. His words still confront our doctrinal battles, our moral confusion, and our selfishness.

> "What causes fights and quarrels among you? Don't they come from your desires that battle within you? You want something but don't get it. You kill and covet, but you cannot have what you want. You quarrel and fight. You do not have, because you do not ask God. When you ask, you do not receive, because you ask with wrong motives, that you may spend what you get on your pleasures. 'You adulterous people, don't you know that friendship with the world is hatred toward God? Anyone who chooses to be a friend of the world becomes an enemy of God. Or do you think Scripture says without reason that the spirit he caused to live in us envies intensely? But he gives us more grace. That is why Scripture says: 'God opposes the proud but gives grace to the humble'" (James 4: 1-6, NIV).

These instructions from the New Testament come from loving teachers. They want the church to understand what dedication means. They have no desire to bully us into commitment. Instead, they want us to know that the proper response when meeting the person and work of Jesus Christ (see chapter 5) is to put everything into Christ's service.

Dedication is a common thread throughout the New Testament letters. For instance, Paul often starts his letters with a detailed description of Christ's work. Once he establishes the authority of Christ, reminding believers they were bought with a price, he boldly states the right response is the dedication of life to Christ. A true love for the Savior models the kind of love the Savior showed total sacrifice of life. This is why Paul wrote: "I appeal to you therefore, brothers and sisters, by the mercies of God, to present your bodies as a living sacrifice, holy and acceptable to God, which is your spiritual worship. Do not be conformed to this world, but be transformed by the renewing of your minds, so that

you may discern what is the will of God-what is good and acceptable and perfect" (Romans 12:1-2, NRSV).

Peter's first letter, too, adds rich detail to an understanding of
dedication. He writes, "But you are a chosen race, a royal priesthood, a holy nation, God's own people, in order that you may proclaim the mighty acts of him who called you out of darkness into
his marvelous light. Once you were not a people, but now you are
God's people once you had not received mercy, but now you have
received mercy" (1 Peter 2:9-10, NRSV, italics mine). These four
titles are ways our dedication shows.

- *A chosen race.* Peter is not writing about Hispanics, Asians,
  Blacks, Caucasians, or any other race/ ethnic body, as superior to the rest. Rather, God has called out a people to live
  toward the peaceable kingdom. We decide to enter God's
  kingdom, but God actively works to strengthen us to make
  the choice. Our choosing and God's choosing are two strands
  of the same rope. Peter's message to us is not to err by thinking God is uninvolved or weak. God actively pursues people,
  and God actively empowers them to choose the kingdom. It
  is the Holy Spirit who fuels whole life dedication, because we
  could not choose God's way if God was not enabling us to do
  so in the first place.

- *A royal priesthood.* The idea of a priestly kingdom starts with
  Moses and continues through Revelation. In the throne room
  of heaven we hear the 24 elders falling before the Lamb singing, "By your blood you ransomed for God saints from every
  tribe and language and people and nation; you have made
  them to be a kingdom and priests serving our God, and they
  will reign on earth" (Revelation 5:9-10). Priests represented
  the ideals of what God's people were to be. They were to live
  as symbols of perpetual worship of the God who chose them.
  They were a tithe of God's people. The priesthood began with
  a public anointing, ritualistic and reverent, just like a king's
  anointing. Aaron and his sons were liberally anointed with
  blood (Exodus 29) and oil (Leviticus 8) as a sign that they

were dedicated to God. Christians who hold to the priest-hood of all believers should appreciate this priestly role. They understand that though some may take on a professional pastoral role, every believer must participate in ministry. We exist to point the way to God, to help a lost and broken world find its way to redemption. We are to represent the ideals of God's people, and live as symbols of perpetual worship of the God who chose us. Our priestly role begins with baptism—public, ritualistic, and reverent. When understood and administered properly, baptism communicates our pledge to walk in God's way as dedicated kingly priests—proclaiming forgiveness and seeking justice.

God provided instructions for how a king must rule over God's people (Deuteronomy 17:14-20):

a. A king was to be a subject of the kingdom, not a foreigner.

b. The king was not to accumulate wealth, military, power, or wives.

c. As king, he was to read God's law daily and become known for his reverence for God's way.

d. The king was not to consider himself more important than other members of God's community (King Lemuel's mother interpreted kingly rule this way—see Proverbs 31: [a] not to have multiple marriage alliances with other kingdoms, [b] not to let his judgment be clouded by wine, and [c] not to pervert the rights of the afflicted. She also told him to [a] give comfort to the suffering, [b] be the voice of the voiceless, [c] be an advocate for the rights of destitute people, and [d] be a just judge.)

This kingly heritage belongs to the dedicated Christian. We are to rule with God in God's way not hoarding wealth, not seeking our own welfare at the expense of others, and becoming advocates for those who have no other hope.

Israel's kings were anointed with oil, a public, ritualistic, and reverent act intended to communicate that they ruled as God's servant, and only at God's pleasure. Many of Israel's and Judah's kings misunderstood this dedication. Perhaps the temptations inherent in access to power and possible wealth distracted them from their kingly purpose Could the North American church be facing similar temptations today?

- *A holy nation.* The word "holy" means the same as dedicated or sanctified. God s nation, this chosen race, this royal priesthood—are a people dedicated to God's purposes. Our existence is to glorify the One who chooses us.

- *God's own people.* God's unique people are not only chosen, or dedicated to divine purposes—we also belong to God. God doesn't just use us. God owns us. Example: My family leases a van. We drive it, but it does not belong to us the way a vehicle belongs when the title sits in our filing cabinet. The dealer and the finance company agreed we had the resources available to dedicate the van to our use for three years, but they have the final say over the van's destiny. We cannot sell it without detailed arrangements with the manufacturer. God doesn't rent, lease, or borrow a people for kingdom purposes. God holds our title of ownership. Our title is filed in the Lamb's book of life, and now we live in service to God.

As a chosen race, a royal priesthood, a holy nation, and God s own people, Peter says our purpose is to proclaim the mighty acts of the One who called us out of darkness and into the marvelous light of God. We make this proclamation by living as agents of healing and hope. Our unique identity and task come from God's extension of mercy to us. Before, we were alienated and had no identity. But God formed us into a people, and showed us mercy. Now we have a name, and a task to proclaim God's work. We accomplish this by living as a chosen nation of kingly priests.

Summary

God, through Jesus Christ, reached out to us and rescued us from our desperate state. If we accept our need and the level of mercy shown us, the Holy Spirit develops in us a deep love for Jesus and strengthens us to dedicate all of our life to the Savior. We then become part of God's people, proclaiming God s mighty acts as a chosen nation of kingly priests, helping to build God's kingdom.

Reflections

Considering what you understand about whole life dedication, what counsel would you give the following people?

a. Josef Scalino is a bricklayer with four children to support. His wife, Rosa, works part-time at a fast-food restaurant to support their income. In a small-group discussion on stewardship, Josef tells the class he figures it is okay for his family to use Rosa's income to purchase a pop-up camper for his family to use on weekends. After all, they give 10 percent of his income to the congregation. What remains is theirs to use as they see fit.

b. Steve Sheldon is a pastor from Warminster, Pennsylvania. He is on an island cruise on the SS Norway. Steve returned to the ship after visiting a private island owned by the cruise line—an island where everything is clean, the water is safe to drink, and the only visitors are vessel passengers like him. A Wall Street Journal reporter approaches Steve and some fellow passengers and asks how they liked the private island in comparison to the island nations they visited while on the cruise. Someone next to Steve says, "St. Maarten wasn't a very attractive island. It was dirty. The shops were kind of junky." Steve adds, 'Jamaica seems pretty run down to us."[4]

4. "Ersatz Isles Lack Local Color, but the Bathrooms Shine." In *The Wall Street Journal* February 16, 1996, B1.

c. Betty and Amos Hollinger live on the first floor of their sprawling family home and survive on a modest fixed income. 78-year-old Amos had a stroke two years ago, and 74-year-old Betty uses up most of her energy caring for him. Betty hasn't been to church during this time because she would have to find someone to watch Amos. Betty doesn't have the courage to ask, and no one has offered. Betty wonders how much longer she can care for Amos by herself, especially since their closest child lives two states away.

d. Jim Fryar is the associate pastor of a 300-member church. He is responsible for the annual class of baptismal candidates. There usually is a group of ten or more high school students. Jim is increasingly discouraged with this process. He often wonders if he adequately conveys the depth necessary for a Christian commitment and whether his students know what a dedicated life entails. He longs for a deeper reason for pursuing baptism other than, "Jesus is . . . like . . . really special, you know."

e. Molly Halverson, a committed Christian, is two weeks from completing a graduate degree. She is undecided between two job offers. Molly spent an internship at a top business company that is now recruiting her aggressively. She knows the ropes, the people, and the responsibilities. It is a perfect fit for her talents. And the generous starting salary shouldn't be taken lightly, especially with the sizable education debt Molly acquired in pursuit of her degree. But Molly was also approached by a church service agency her uncle supports. They want her to become the executive director and help them develop a strategic plan. The salary is small.

f. DeWayne and Linda Beatty have been relating to their non-Christian neighbors, Wally and Alice Horn. Their children attend the same school so there has been plenty of opportunity for pizza bashes and ice cream cones after athletic contests and band concerts. DeWayne and Linda have not been particularly overt about their faith; neither have they hidden it. Now Wally invited De Wayne to breakfast at a local diner. They find a booth, sit down, and order. As the waitress leaves, Wally leans forward and says, "DeWayne, I know you are a church fellow and all. I'd like someone to tell me once and for all what being a Christian is. As I listen to the news or those television preachers, I get all sorts of notions. What does your church teach?" How would you answer?

g. Beatrice Dyck is a missionary in an East African country. Her mission agency pays her a wage far superior to any East African friend she has. For the past eighteen months Beatrice employed a maid, mostly because the woman had been living in utter poverty and had three children to support. Beatrice feels guilty paying her maid the average wage, or even for having a maid in the first place. But she knows if she let the maid go, she would have no work, or if she paid her more, the maid's spending power would outpace that of her community. Besides, what would happen when Beatrice returned home and the maid had to find another job at a much lower wage?

Suggestions

a. List three critical issues that face your congregation What obstacles to mission seem to get constantly in the way? Compare your list with the list given in James 4:1-6. Do you find any matches? What does James suggest?

b. Tell additional stories you know of people forced to choose between a tyrant and Christ. Speculate on what those people might say to today's North American church about a life that is dedicated to Christ.

c. Write down your understanding of dedication, and list ways your life shows it. Are there undedicated aspects to your life? If so, what needs to happen for you to give them to Jesus? Reflect on the mighty acts of God that stand out the most to you—both from the Bible and personal experience. What propels you to share God's mighty acts with others? What holds you back from being a proclaimer?

d. In a Sunday school class, or with a friend, discuss how the concept of God owning you strikes you. Are you comfortable with it? Does it trouble you in some way? Elaborate.

7

Firstfruits Living

Belief: We show this dedication when we give back to God out of the first and best of the resources we manage on God's behalf, and by managing the rest in generous ways that give glory to God.

BECAUSE WE BELIEVE OUR use of money communicates our values, we harness the power of money to that end. Our values are rooted in God's character, and are seen in the person and work of Jesus Christ. As we experience God's deep grace through Jesus, we gladly dedicate all of life, including money, to God's purposes. This chapter is concerned with how we use money to reflect our dedication.

Firstfruits Living

Firstfruits giving was recorded in Genesis when Cain and Abel brought an offering to the Lord. Abel, in particular, was blessed for bringing his gift from the first and best of his crops (Genesis 4:4). Here is an overview of how gifts were used in the Bible:

Old Testament

When God separated Abraham from the surrounding nations and began a lasting covenant with him, wealth was not based on currency, but in bearing sons. Sons kept land ownership and livestock in the family. Daughters-in-law brought dowry, usually in the form of flocks and herds, to the husband's family. The bigger the family, the greater its potential wealth. Ancient peoples believed males were mainly responsible for producing male heirs. They thought a man carried the complete seed for human life within his testes. In order to establish a covenant, God asked Abraham, and all sons to follow, to dedicate the instrument believed to be the source of wealth. Abraham did this when he was 99, with only God's promise that a son would finally come (Genesis 17:16). And even when the son came, God asked Abraham to demonstrate his commitment to their covenant by offering his firstborn back in an act of worship (Genesis 22).

- After Abraham's descendants grew into a nation and experienced slavery, Moses became God's instrument to plan for Hebrew society. The center of this new nation's government and economy was the tithe. God's people set aside a tithe from the firstfruits of their harvest and flocks. They ate none of their harvest until the firstfruits offering was made (Leviticus 23:14). They brought these fruits and animals to the tabernacle and ate a meal made from their tithe, to demonstrate their own dedication as a people (Deuteronomy 14:22ff.; 15:19ff.). The leftover portions of sacrificed grain and meat became food for priests and their families (Deuteronomy 14:27). The priests then offered to God their tithe of Israel's tithe, and then ate it in God's presence, as did the rest of Israel (Numbers 18:25-32).

- Every third year, the tithe was brought to a community storehouse instead of God's house. This was for Levites, widows, orphans, and aliens who lived among God's people (Deuteronomy 14:28-29; 26:1-15). These groups had no inheritance in the land of Canaan, and were dependent on these systematic gifts for their livelihood.

- The tithe was more than a predetermined percentage of one's income. Firstfruits offerings were made of the firstborn of all cattle (Numbers 18:8ff.). The priests and Levites were set aside as a tithe of Israel's population (Numbers 8:14-19). Even the firstborn child was to be dedicated to God, literally bought back with a money purchase, since Israel did not sacrifice its children (Numbers 18:15). In other words, all of Israel's bounty belonged to God, a God-given inheritance (Deuteronomy 26: 1, 2). Firstfruits giving was a discipline to remind them who owned all.

- Firstfruits offerings were to be celebrations. All family members attended. Wine or stronger drink accompanied the feast. Retelling of God's mighty acts and promises of faithfulness to the covenant was part of the merriment (Deuteronomy 14:22-27; 26:1-15).

New Testament

- Jesus criticized the Pharisees for taking a legalistic approach to tithing while neglecting weightier matters of justice, mercy, and faith, which tithing should have funded (Matthew 23:23).

- Matthew 25 is a clear call for Christians to care for the hungry, the thirsty, the stranger, the naked, the ill, and the prisoner, an expectation derived from the Old Testament covenant. From the rest of Scripture's teachings we understand that doing these things does not get anyone into heaven, but that those going to heaven do these things (Ephesians 2:8-10).

- The earliest offerings in the New Testament church are described at the end of Acts 2 and 4. Donations were used for daily love feasts and care for needy people. The opening verses of Acts 6 describe the church's continued concern for widows. Barnabas and others sold land and donated the proceeds (Acts 4:34).

- Paul wrote the most detailed instructions about giving in the New Testament (see 1 Corinthians 16:1-4 as well as 2 Corinthians 8-9). He collected offerings to relieve the sufferings of other Christians, especially the persecuted Jerusalem church.

He also instructed the church to be generous with church servants who were set aside to engage in the church's ministry as their livelihood (1 Timothy 5:17-18; see also Hebrews 13:17).

- James provides some of the most direct statements about the church and its donations. For him, pure religion means caring for widows and orphans as much as it means personal holiness (James 2:27). He also restates the teaching of Jesus about care for naked, hungry, and homeless people (James 2:14-17; see also Hebrews 13:1-3).

- The writings of Peter, Paul, James, and John emphasize the same teachings. We are blessed with all spiritual blessings, adopted as God's children, redeemed through Christ's blood, forgiven of our sins, lavished with God's grace, informed of God's mysterious will, given an inheritance that enables us to live to God's glory, and marked with the seal of the Holy Spirit as a foretaste of blessings to come (Ephesians 1 :3-14). Because of God's great gifts to us, a firstfruits lifestyle reflects the bounty we received (2 Corinthians 8:6-12).

God's people brought their first and best to their places of worship. The money or goods were used first for celebration feasts, then for care of ministering people, and then for the support of needy people in the community. We become generous, not just with our firstfruits gifts, but in our lifestyle, because we have been treated generously. Firstfruits living means we move away from individual use of money and possessions—we no longer see the money as "ours" alone—and we move toward a growing generosity in all of life. No longer are we consumers, but blessing-givers. We become generous with the families we are part of, and we become generous with the widows, orphans, aliens, naked, hungry, thirsty, imprisoned, and ill in our lives. We don't do it because it is our duty. We do it because we cannot not do it!

Church Budgets

Stewardship in general should never be linked to "meeting the budget." Budgets are a human invention for following through with the program a church decides it wants to do. A budget is not a divine mandate. Budget shortfalls tempt well-intentioned wealthy people to step out of the rhythmic discipline of worshiping God by waiting to make up the difference. It leads less wealthy people to think their giving is complete once they contribute "their fair share." People struggling financially sometimes conclude that since they can't contribute "their fair share," why should they participate in giving firstfruits? The danger is that meeting a budget replaces the act of worship that giving is supposed to be. Churches are wise to manage funds collected in worship. Churches are unwise, though, to substitute business procedure for an act of worship. Budgeting simply does not appear in the Bible. Giving was an act of worship, a celebration. Let's return giving to its rightful place!

What firstfruits giving can mean for North American Christians

Giving firstfruits to God is a celebration.

Old Testament firstfruits giving were feasts. The New Testament talked about cheerful giving. What would happen if congregations across North America began to treat their offerings as such? Instead of giving offerings to God, they could receive offerings for God. Instead of a commercial in the midst of worship where an offering plate gets passed, the offering could become a high point of worship as the entire congregation participates m celebrating God's bounty. The offering could become a time for worship leaders to recount God's faithful acts. People would check to be sure everyone around them had something to give. Plates would be passed high in the air, or people would stream forward in a parade of generosity. As offering plates are passed, people could also be given opportunity to offer their time or talents as a contribution to the Lord's work. When ushers are needed, they could reflect the diversity of the congregation. When the offering plates are brought to the front of the church, worship leaders would dedicate the offerings to God's purposes. They would lift the plates heavenward, proclaim the congregation's love for God, and tell God how the offering will be used to help build the kingdom.

We get to share with God in the use of firstfruits.

It's okay for us to share in the bounty! God's people have always used offerings to build houses of worship, and to share in fellowship feasts together. God joins a dedicated people at these meals and in these buildings. God expects us to participate with the divine intention to give abundant life to all. The offerings a congregation receives should help pastors serve the church, adequately provide for their families, and be generous givers themselves. A congregation's offerings also need to continue the tradition of relieving the suffering of widows, orphans, strangers, sick, hungry, thirsty and imprisoned people around the world. God doesn't magically suck money from offering plates and rain it back down on needy people. God uses us. We are the points of distribution. We use the inheritance we received as a trust to manage in God's behalf, according to God's values.

Giving demonstrates our whole life dedication.

Christians are people who decided to embrace God's great generosity. In that embrace, more and more of our life becomes dedicated to God, including our wealth. A firstfruits lifestyle grows out of this whole life dedication.

Summary

We show our dedication to God through living a firstfruits lifestyle. This means we give to God out of the first and best of the resources we manage on God's behalf. This also means we anticipate sharing in God's generosity as we manage the rest of those resources. We move away from individual use of money and possessions and towards growing generosity in all of life—to our families, to God's servants, and to the needy. In all of our giving we celebrate God's faithfulness to us.

Reflections

How do the following people understand dedication of money? Based on the material of this chapter, how are they correct? Where are they mistaken?

a. Barry Peters is in the plumbing and heating business. He can maintain a middle-class lifestyle only because he lives in an area with a low cost of living. Each year, Barry sits down to calculate what his church contribution should be based upon a per-member formula. Since the congregation's budget jumped to $125,000 this year, and there are fifty families, Barry figures he owes $2,500. The problem is, last year's budget was $110,000, and Barry's earnings will not keep pace with the increase. Barry intends to complain about the increase at the members' meeting next week.

b. Patricia Meek feels the church has not spent enough on missions. When her congregation set out to do a building project, because the main structure could not service the more than 150 people who attended each Sunday morning, Patricia started giving her gift directly to the mission board of her denomination. If and when the church starts giving missions its proper due, will she give to missions through her congregation again?

c. Simone and Jerry Flores recently complained to their pastor that they cannot understand why so much money goes outside the congregation to organizations they know nothing about. "Why do we give to places we can't see or touch? Why do we give so much to others and don't pay attention to needs inside the church?" Jerry and Simone have two active preschoolers, and wish the church would put a "cry room" at the back of the sanctuary. This would allow them to take a disruptive toddler out of the congregation, but still witness the worship service. They told their pastor that more of their friends with young children would come to church if such a room was available. They also said that if the church agreed to provide a cry room, they would pledge a substantial gift to help make it possible.

d. Regina Marcum remembers that a pastor embezzled some money from the congregation she grew up in. Now she no longer trusts churches as a place to be faithful to God with her money. Regina set up an automatic deduction of 10 percent of each paycheck as a donation to several community service organizations.

e. Suzy Dashan is a new deacon, and is she ever excited! She didn't know just how much her congregation gave to help needy people until she started serving in her deacon's role. She didn't know how much other churches in the community looked to her congregation as an example of God's grace. Before becoming a deacon, Suzy contributed about 2 percent of her income to her congregation. In the past three months, however, she doubled her contributions to the congregation, and often gives out of her pocket to some of the needy to whom she ministers.

f. Bob and Sarah Waidner believe God blessed them with financial prosperity. They give 3 percent of their income to the congregation's budget each week. They also give generously to mission or building fund appeals on top of that. Combined with giving to community groups and their college alma maters, their charitable giving averages 9-11 percent of their annual income.

g. Betty Schrock couldn't care less about tax-deductible contributions. She is dependent on her deceased husband's small pension and a social security pittance. She has not owed any income tax in five years. She puts an occasional five-dollar bill in the offering plate for a traveling preacher who isn't afraid to get a bit excited.

h. A group of citizens in Colorado put together an amendment to end property tax exemptions for nonprofit groups that do not provide housing for prisoners, orphans, the elderly, the disabled, and the homeless. While not likely to become law, churches and other nonprofit organizations are lobbying to fight the amendment's passage. Interestingly enough, there is no report of churches or other nonprofits scrambling to provide housing for prisoners, orphans, the elderly, the disabled, and the homeless in order to remain tax-free.[1]

Suggestions

a. Invite a Sunday school class or small group to engage in a detailed study of Genesis 15-17. Note what God intended to provide Abraham and Sarah's descendants, how it would be provided, and what God intended to do through their vast family.

b. Evaluate how your congregation treats offerings during the church service. Do you "take" offerings or "receive" them? Are they dedicated to God in any way? Do they celebrate God's gifts? How does your congregation maximize the participation of those gathered in worship?

c. Evaluate the destination of your congregation's income. What percentage is used for building maintenance and supplies (including custodial salaries)? What percentage pays for the local ministry of the church (including ministry staff expenses)? What percentage goes to worldwide concerns? What percentage would you estimate is self-serving? What percentage goes to assist hungry, thirsty, naked, imprisoned, widowed, displaced, or orphaned people? Does the use of

1. Christianity Today, March 4, 1996, 74.

your congregation's finances demonstrate the threefold priority of celebrating God's goodness, providing for those who minister professionally, and helping the needy?

d. Write your definition of firstfruits giving. Invite others from your church fellowship to assist you. What percentage do you believe constitutes a tithe? Should the entire gift go to the congregation? Or do you have individual say over how this money should be used?

e. Volunteer to help your congregation receive an offering. How about composing a worship service built around a celebration of offering? Use some of the ideas found in this chapter.

8

Our First Family

Belief: When we make decisions about generous and grace-filled living, we who received the Holy Spirit are inspired to seek the counsel of the church—our family of greatest importance.

BECAUSE OF THE CONSTANT temptation to move away from a whole-life dedication, we need the Holy Spirit working in the church family to help us be accountable. Our best decisions about living generously are made with the help of other people seeking to be fully dedicated to God. This chapter considers five Bible passages that make this point.

The believers share their possessions: Acts 4:32-5:7

The early believers' tremendous spirit of generosity was fueled by God's grace (Acts 4:33). Possessions were willingly shared. The gospel was powerfully preached. The needy were taken care of, and the financial burden of ministry was supplied through proceeds from real-estate sales. This generosity was exemplified by Barnabas (a/k/a Joseph) who sold a field and put the money at the apostles' feet.

But Ananias and Sapphira (Acts 5:1-10) missed the point of whole-life dedication. They pretended to donate all the money from a land sale, but secretly kept some back for their own use. Their actions brought about their death, not because they kept some of the money—they had every right to do so—but because they lied to God and their church community about it.

From this story, we can make several observations about money accountability within the church. *First,* the church had some idea of who was giving what. Years after the event, Luke knew Barnabas made his contribution and recorded it for posterity. This doesn't mean these gifts were made public with great fanfare, but giving was not secretive, either.

The early church struggled to find a balance between publicity and humility in giving. When Jesus said our giving should be done in secret (Matthew 6:4), he was not so much blessing secretive giving as he was condemning those who pretended they were righteous because they gave. Ananias and Sapphira, however, sought notoriety and spirituality in connection with the gift. Their harsh punishment shows that false spirituality has no place in the church. Totally private giving can present the same dangers—letting us pretend we give even when we do not. Battling false spirituality is the point of the instructions of Jesus and Luke's story, far more than telling us to give in private.

A *second* observation is that the early church saw their earning potential as individuals as gifts to give to the believing community. Earning more allowed them to be that much more generous. North American Christians, by contrast, tend to use extra income to accumulate and to consume instead of to increase generosity. Statistical studies show that the greater the wage, the lower the percentage of income that gets donated to charity. North Americans practice proportional selfishness rather than proportional giving.

In contrast, Luke's story in Acts 4 tells of one church where there was subtle pressure for members to give rather than accumulate. The pressure was maintained through their experience of God's grace, their openness to the Spirit, their common life, their fervent evangelism, and their direct connection to those they served. If our
churches today wish to fuel lifetime generosity and also to promote mutual financial accountability, they are wise to study the experience of the first-century Christians.

Generosity encouraged: 2 Corinthians 8: 1-15

When Paul was raising funds for the impoverished and suffering church in Jerusalem, he set up a friendly contribution competition between the Corinthian and the Macedonian churches. He apologized only a little when he wrote, "I do not mean that there should be relief for others and pressure on you, but it is a question of a fair balance between your present abundance and their need, so that their abundance may be for your need, in order that there may be a fair balance. As it is written, 'The one who had much did not have too much, and the one who had little did not have too little'" (2 Corinthians 8:13-15, NRSV). We can draw at least two lessons from this passage:

First, church leaders have the right to ask members to be generous, even to apply a little pressure to make good on our commitments. For example, as Paul's fund raising campaign got underway, he invited people to set aside a weekly sum in keeping with their income (1 Corinthians 16:1-4). In this way, a giving discipline developed and few additional appeals were needed. The amount was apparently left up to the individual, although Paul strongly encouraged proportional giving. It was not until his second letter that he applied pressure. Apparently the Corinthians were finding it difficult to follow through on their commitment to help the suffering church at Jerusalem. Churches with abundance should not hoard it. Churches who were persecuted and shut out of the economic systems of their region needed relief. Paul's role as a church leader was to teach generosity among churches, and see that the contributions were administered.

Many North American congregations have stripped leadership of this important role. Pastors feel powerless to talk about money, especially when a church is behind in giving to the vision to which it committed itself. They know the criticism that comes if they strongly remind the congregation to continue in generosity. One solution is for pastors to infuse stewardship teaching into all of congregational life, not just on special stewardship Sundays. Doing so lets church members hear about more than raising money for specific church endeavors, and they are more likely to respond with joy than out of guilt.

A *second* lesson is our responsibility to care for congregations other than our own. Through a shift toward localized funding of ministry, North American Christianity is losing its ability to provide systematic long-term assistance for medical, nutritional, educational, and spiritual needs. Our motivation is now focused on helping those close by, and then only when a special appeal is made. But we are members of a global Christian family, full of need *and* full of abundance. We must help each other when in need, and we must also encourage each other to be generous when we experience abundance.

Doing good to all: Galatians 6: 1-5

These verses do not say anything directly about the Christian community and money, but we can infer some instruction about helping one another remain faithful in money matters.

First, when a believer sins by letting love of money take God's place, the goal of mature Christians should be their gentle restoration (v. l).

Second, those responsible for restoring a believer caught in sin should be careful to avoid the temptation of materialism themselves (v. 1).

Third, believers should accept the responsibility to share the burdens of other Christians. This follows the law of Christ-to love a neighbor who makes selfish financial decisions just as much as we love ourselves (v. 2).

Fourth, Christians should not use the restoration of someone from financial sin as an opportunity to compare themselves to the sinner and thereby take pride in their economic maturity. Christians should test their own economic decisions against the standards to which they are pledged (w. 3-4).

Note the two-edged sword in the second instruction. Materialism is a pitfall for the wealthy, the frugal, and even the poor. The problem with having money, or not having money, is that it can easily become more important than people or God's kingdom. Whether we overspend, or spend our lives figuring how *not* to spend, it

adds up to materialism.

Instructions for God's servant: 1 Timothy 6:11-16; 2 Timothy 4:1-5

In these passages, Paul instructs the young church leader, Timothy, to flee from the love of money and instead to pursue righteousness, godliness, faith, love, endurance, and gentleness. According to Paul, we pledge ourselves to move toward God and away from the materialistic world's offerings when we confess our faith in the presence of the congregation. Once again, Paul as church leader authoritatively provides instruction in the realm of money. And once again we see the church, the gathered community of dedicated ones, as the touchstone of economic accountability.

> Materialism is a pitfall tor the wealthy, the frugal, and even the poor. The problem with having money, or *not* having money, is that it can easily become more important than people or God's kingdom. Whether we overspend, or spend our lives figuring how not to spend, it adds up to materialism.

Paul warns Timothy that a time is coming when people will surround themselves with teachers and teachings that say only what they want to hear and offer no challenge for spiritual maturity. Paul says, "They will turn their ears away from the truth and turn aside to myths" (2 Timothy 4:4, NIV). This is exactly what people do when they love money more than God. Church leaders have the responsibility to call the congregation to discern the will of the Holy Spirit in all their actions, including their use of money.

Gene Getz said it well:

> "Since . . . you can tell more about a person's spiritual life by reading through his checkbook ledger than by almost any other means, it is paramount that we Christians

instruct each other in regard to the biblical management of our resources."[1]

God comes first

The Christian covenant requires a supreme allegiance to God that can cost even our human family. Jesus said, "Whoever comes to me and does not hate father and mother, wife and children, brothers and sisters, yes, and even life itself, cannot be my disciple" (Luke 14:26, NRSV). Mary Stewart Van Leeuwen asserts:

> "Jesus' own life and teachings underscore the fact that marriage and family now take back seat to the universal proclamation of God's salvation and the formation of a new first family—a worldwide kingdom building company, in which membership depends not at all on bloodlines, but on faith in the Messiah."[2]

She continues:

> "The radical mistake of the human race is that of pushing God into second or third or last place . . . of giving a higher value to other goals than to the purpose of God." [Writes Bromily . . .] In doing so, ironically, humans lose the means by which those other goals, including marriage and family, can become most satisfying. For it is only by making God's kingdom their primary commitment that humans avoid worshiping the created, rather than the Creator, 'a sure recipe for disappointment in the end.'"[3]

Certainly, congregations have much work to do to strengthen a commitment to the church family. Yet we are promised a Helper, an Advocate, for this costly discipleship. We are also blessed with the companionship of others who also participate in this

---

1. Taken from: Getz, *A Biblical Theology of Material Possessions*, 11. Copyright 1990, Moody Bible Institute of Chicago. Moody Press. Used by permission.

2. Bromily, *Gender and Grace*, 173–74.

3. Ibid., 174.

all-consuming covenant. Together, single and married can learn that a covenant to be part of Christ's kingdom is not merely a covenant to receive God's grace, but to be an extension of it. This means we come to church, not just expecting to get, but to give. The sons and daughters of families in the congregation become sons and daughters of the whole Christian community. Newcomers are the responsibility of the whole family, not just of those who brought them. We no longer expect to be on the receiving end of the church's work, but to be an integral part of it. After all, we belong to God's kingdom!

Summary

The strong temptation that accompanies money means we need help to be accountable for continued generous living. Since the church is a community of dedicated individuals and also an extension of the kingdom that holds our highest loyalty, the church becomes the place for accountability. Church leadership can provide sound instruction on what it means to be Christian in the use of money. Church members should invite the Holy Spirit's leading to help one another avoid monetary sin. Church members should also use any abundance of money to strengthen places where the church has great need. In the midst of this giving and receiving counsel, Christians should be quick to bear the burdens of others and refrain from deciding who is being the most faithful. Our dedication to God comes first. This may be costly, but a church family guided by the Holy Spirit can strengthen and guide us for generous living.

Reflections

How would you help the following Christian people talk to each other, in light of the insights you gained from this chapter?

a. Janeen Carter is the mayor of a small city of 30,000. Recent immigration of a distinct ethnic group has raised significant racial tension, primarily because they "don't speak English," "steal jobs away from people," and "live off the welfare system." Janeen knows most of these comments are severely distorted, but social services throughout the city are strapped. Matters are complicated further by two dynamics that shrink the tax base. *First,* many of the city's middle to upper middle class are selling their homes and building new ones outside the city limits. Many of the homes are converted into multi-family rentals and property values decline. As a result the city collects less property tax from fewer people. *Second,* the city has a growing population of seniors, many of whom belong to a concentration of churches from a single denomination. The denomination operates a large nonprofit senior citizen complex inside the city limits. The complex provides housing options from condominium living to fully assisted long-term care. Many of the city's seniors are on a waiting list to get into the complex, and new construction is underway to accommodate them. Because it is a nonprofit organization, no property taxes are paid, either by the residents or the corporation. Henry Wiens is the CEO of the senior citizen complex. He has already overseen five expansion projects and still the list grows. Given the community's demographics, it is reasonable to expect a 40 percent increase in demands over the next fifteen years. Tonight, Henry will sit down with Mayor Carter and a few key people from the city zoning board to negotiate for 40 acres of city-owned property.

b. Garry Johnson makes $60,000 a year at his sales manager job. Garry's expertise led to his appointment on his church's board. They want to send him to an all-expenses paid denominational training session 400 miles away. Garry books a flight, and since the conference ends Saturday afternoon, Garry skips the cheaper Saturday night stay in order to get home sooner. Garry doesn't like to be away any longer than is necessary, since his job already requires him to travel more than 100 days per year. Raoul Suarez makes $27,000 a year from his three part-time jobs. Raoul wants to attend the same training session, but will have to take a vacation day and pay expenses out of his own pocket to attend. The small congregation he attends has no funds for anything like this, although they did take an offering that provided 75 percent of Raoul's bus fare. The last time Raoul left his inner-city community was three years ago, when his sister got married.

c. The Central Village Church has a policy of paying the tuition of any child of a church member who attends the local Christian high school. The tuition is a budget line item based on the number of students from the congregation. Because Central Village Church attracts a number of families with high school age children, and because the cost of a Christian high school education continues to climb the tuition fund now dominates the congregation's budget. Each year, a tense discussion breaks out between those who think the program should continue and those who think private education is a luxury the church should not reinforce. Those supporting the program either have high schoolers, or recently did. Most of those opposing the tuition aid program have no children enrolled.

d. Faye Stepien has pulled off three wonderful Christmas banquets for the church on a minimal budget. This past December was the best one yet. Somehow she produced a three-meat buffet out of a local banquet hall, complete with first-class entertainment, for $15 a head. She is especially proud of her church's tradition of not letting this be a couple's only event. Singles and children come, too. Many people went out of their way to praise Faye for her hard work. During open mike time at a congregational business meeting a few weeks later, Sammy Frazee complained about the high cost of church events like these: "I'm the only one earning income for my family of four," he said. "One event like this blows what we set aside for entertainment each month. Can't we just have a potluck at the church and skip the paid entertainment? I appreciate the fact that some loving people have paid the way for my family for the past two years, but I want a solution that doesn't obligate someone to give my family charity, or that tempts us to expect it."

e. Jake Moynihan is a financial consultant specializing in mutual funds that develop the infrastructure of "underdeveloped" countries. He likes helping people improve their world through socially responsible investing, while increasing their wealth. His favorite verse is Ecclesiastes 11:1: "Send out your bread upon the waters, for after many days you will get it back." Jake is just about to leave for a special Sunday evening service at his church. Beverly Rice, the speaker for the evening and a rural development worker in Bolivia, is putting the finishing touches on her notes. Her text is Matthew 6: 19 and following: "Do not store up for yourselves treasures on earth . . . " Beverly intends to focus on the immediate needs many people have just to survive, needs that don't wait for hydroelectric plants and meaningful jobs. She intends to be gentle, yet prophetic—calling people to do with less so that others might live.

f. The Franz family is serious about their financial accountability resting in their local congregation, but as they consider purchasing their next vehicle they are reluctant to bring it to their small group for advice. They are afraid that they will be misunderstood. Barry Cooper, one member of the small group, always harps on the wastefulness of purchasing new cars and letting a dealership do all the servicing. "I put at least 200,000 miles on every car I've ever owned," he says. "Did most of my own mechanical work, too." But neither Tim nor Sally Franz has much mechanical ability, and their jobs require a lot of driving. They wonder whether asking for advice might be too much of a relational risk.

Suggestions

a. Plan a retreat for eight to twelve people in which you will focus on writing and sharing personal money autobiographies in a nonjudgmental and prayerful atmosphere. Study some of the Scriptures discussed in this book during common worship times.

b. For your own reflection write several case studies based on experiences from your life. In particular, write about those where you witnessed different economic perspectives at play between two or more Christians. Invite others to discuss them with you.

c. Brainstorm ways you are willing to share the concerns of your Christian sisters and brothers, especially those with economic burdens. Develop a plan to follow through.

d. Working with others, outline a process for restoring someone mired in monetary sin. List the types of monetary sins Christians might fall into, and discuss how confrontation, restoration, and healing should take place.

e. Evaluate how your congregation works with different economic perspectives in the church. Are people free to talk about money or are they secretive? Does church leadership have freedom to instruct with authority on the subject of money? Are people with different perspectives on economic issues and money able to talk with each other with mutual respect?

9

Seven Initiatives for Congregations

AT A LUNCHEON FOR pastors, a table placard suggested those seated at the table share how their congregation passed the offering plate. Glenda O'Malley from Suburban Community Church was the first to notice the card, so she led off, asking everyone to go clockwise around the table. "We don't take offerings," Glenda said proudly. "We don't want people to think we want members just for their money. We have an offering box at the back of the sanctuary, and put an announcement in each week's bulletin that visitors and nonmembers are not expected to contribute. Members put their gifts in the box as they are able and in private. After all, we're not supposed to let our left hand know what our right hand is doing."

Peter Connor spoke next: "At First Church, we have elected ushers—male and female—who serve staggered four-year terms. Our ushers also serve as greeters on Sunday mornings. We usually take our offerings just after the sermon and before the announcements."

The new pastor at Chosen Community Tabernacle, Charley Harness, spoke up: "At CCT, we tell everyone up front how much money is needed each week. If we don't get it we take more offerings until enough money is donated. Just before I came three months ago, the church board voted to have only stable married men over forty years of age act as ushers. For security reasons, we take the offering immediately to the church office and put it in the safe."

Katy and Franklin Warner-Seabolt described their offerings at Faith Fellowship. "If there is a continuum for offering methods, we are probably at the end opposite of Chosen Community," Franklin said. Katy added, "We pass around a sign-up sheet to all members. Families, including children, volunteer to serve as greeters/ushers on a quarterly basis. Whenever a Sunday remains unfilled, we tap a couple of single adults to help us out.

Dr. Jurgen of Downtown Cathedral was seated next to Katy. "The Cathedral has a long history of our deacons serving as ushers. After all, they are the money ministers of the church. We make a big deal of it. Our deacons tend to be retired gentlemen who also help us serve communion to our many shut-ins. The church provides each of them a tuxedo to wear on Sunday mornings, and a fresh boutonniere each week. They are a real class act. Our newcomers always comment on the unique spirit our deacons generate."

The last to speak was Andrew Jones, pastor and founder of Beulah Church: "Offerings for us are a celebration. We don't need anyone to serve as ushers. Our people dance to the front of the church waving their money in the air and singing one of our many offering songs at the top of their lungs. Before the offering begins each week, I remind the church to be faithful to the One who's always faithful to them."

Introducing the Giving Project

Just then, the chair of the Ministerial Council introduced the luncheon speaker. " Murielle Yoder is a consultant with The Giving Project, a project subtitled 'Growing Faithful Stewards in the Church.' Prior to taking on the
consulting role, Murielle was on the pastoral staff of First Mennonite for seven years. Murielle, we look forward to your input at today's luncheon."

Murielle turned her wireless microphone on, came out from behind the lectern, and began speaking. "Thanks for inviting me to describe the seven congregational initiatives The Giving Project uses to develop church communities of generous stewards. Let me make it clear that The Giving Project is not a fundraising organization. Rather, we work to raise a permanent level of generosity in believers—a generosity rooted in a gratitude response to a merciful God. "Most of you have probably heard countless stewardship talks on the three T's-time, talent, treasure—as if they were equal partners in stewardship. But it is The Giving Project's conviction that money has a unique, godlike power that other areas we steward do not have. Nothing else consumes our thinking like money. Nothing else fosters such secrecy or such power. Not sex. Not relationships. Not anything. Because money competes with the very God of heaven, we must come to understand how our use of money communicates what we really care about, no matter what else we say. For disciples of Jesus to be faithful with money, then, they must turn it into a messenger of God's values."

Murielle put a PowerPoint slide up onto the screen. "Here is a diagram of the core beliefs about money that The Giving Project holds. I've mentioned the *first* already—that money is so powerful, and that our use of it communicates what we value.

"*Second*, Christians share God's values. They make the choice to be citizens of God's kingdom, and are loyal to the values of this kingdom. Ideally, they will use money to serve kingdom purposes.

"*Third*, God's values all culminate in this: restoring the universe to its intended purpose-a place of abundant life, a place without suffering, a place where people get to enjoy the fruits of their labor, a place without oppression, or death, or grief, or poverty. Christians respond by using money to help God provide abundant life for all.

"*Fourth*, we believe Jesus, as our Christ and Lord of the universe, is where we meet God's generosity. Jesus is our best Example of how to live out all these values.

"*Fifth*, as we embrace Jesus as the Christ and Lord of the universe, we dedicate all of life to him and want to help God build this kingdom.

"This dedication includes our money, as the *sixth* box shows. We give back to God out of the first and best of all we have been given, and manage the rest in generous ways that give glory to God.

"*Finally,* given money's power and the constant temptation to move away from a whole-life dedication, we need the Holy Spirit and the church family to help us be accountable. Our best decisions about living generously are made with the help of other people seeking to be fully dedicated to God."

Murielle faced the audience. "We're talking about whole life dedication-including dedication of money. We give to God from the first and best of the resources entrusted to us, and we manage the rest in ways that give God glory. In this North American culture of wealth, whole-life dedication requires a patient and deliberate effort. What I am about to describe to you is not a microwave oven approach. This is a careful cultivation of generous communities of faithful stewards."

Cultivating Faithful Stewards-Seven Initiatives

Murielle advanced to the next PowerPoint slide. "Each of you has a number written on masking tape near your place setting. We intentionally sat seven people to a table so that each of you has an opportunity to reflect on how a specific initiative might impact on your congregation. Take a moment to locate the piece of tape near you, then look back up here."

After the bustle to locate numbers, Murielle continued. "Here are seven initiatives The Giving Project recommends to cultivate a community of generous Christians. I'm only going to highlight. Feel free to look at the details in a copy of the congregational manual on the table in the back. After describing the first initiative, I'll give those of you with number one written on your piece of tape one minute to respond to those at your table. After I describe the second initiative, those with number two will have time for a one-minute response, and so on. Use your minute to tell the people at your table what you think would happen if you tried this in your congregation.

"As we get started let's note two things. *First,* this is a systematic approach. Those of us connected with The Giving Project often talk about the church as a stew. When you begin adding new ingredients like a deliberate stewardship cultivation process, you might damage the stew if you don't adjust all the other ingredients.

"*Second,* some of these initiatives are cosmetic. That is, they require the congregation to do a tune-up, or to adapt to some changes most will find easy to embrace. But you might find the other initiatives as hard as training for an Olympic marathon after thirty years as a couch potato. That is why we provide consultants to help you carefully plan a three-to-five-year process for embedding these changes in your congregation's life. In this way, you have a far greater chance for new believers and the children who grow up in your congregation to fully understand the extent of God's grace through Jesus, and also to understand the proper response to that grace."

Initiative One-Resources for Pastors

Murielle advanced the slide and said, "We want pastors to have an adequate grasp of a Christian belief system about money, and be aware that it impacts on their lives too. As spiritual leaders of the congregation, it is imperative that their whole lives are dedicated, including their money, and that they are good financial managers. We start right there.

"Other resources for pastors include aids to preach and teach about money with more authority, and more often. Pastors from congregations who participate in The Giving Project attend a Giving Project Gathering where they are helped to preach more stewardship applications instead of more stewardship sermons. This training is especially helpful in preaching to congregations whose members have diverse economic backgrounds. Pastors also get instructions on leading the church as it makes money decisions. We even convince pastors it's worthwhile to know the giving patterns of church members as a window into their spiritual walk."

Murielle advanced to a blank slide, saying, "Number ones, you have one minute!"

Dr. Jurgen repositioned himself in his chair. "I'm 63 years old, and my economic picture will change next year when I retire. I wonder if The Giving Project isn't thinking more about helping pastors who intend to be around for a while, rather than ones looking to retirement. Her idea about preaching stewardship applications is intriguing though. I figure I have 58 sermons left to preach at the cathedral. I wouldn't mind using these sermons to be more effective in connecting Christian faith to money, especially for the many wealthy people who are part of our congregation. This piece about knowing the giving patterns of my congregation leaves me anxious. I think I want to hear her rationale before commenting more."

Initiative Two-Dedicating Offerings

Murielle broke in above the din. "Let's move on to initiative number two-dedicating offerings. Many congregations take the offering instead of receiving it. They use it as a commercial break instead of as a sacramental act. At best it is an unthinking ritual to meet the church's budget. We make a quick prayer over it, with churchy background music. At worst, the offering has no connection at all with why we gather to worship God. We do it just because that's what you do at church.

"The Giving Project offers resources for churches to receive an offering, to make it a weekly worship celebration where we offer the first and best of our incomes alongside our talents and our time. We help worship leaders learn to dedicate an offering, to lift it up to God and offer it as a response to God's grace. We talk about where to put offering in the order of worship, how to use the offering

as a reminder of our beliefs about Christians and money, and how to create a relationship between the gift giver and the gift receiver.

"Here is one example of an offering prayer provided in the congregational manual, Teaching a Christian View of Money (see resource 5, number 11):

"Great God (lift the offering plates toward heaven),

"These gifts represent the first and best of the resources we have from you.

"We want you to have them.

"The Smith family who work with AIDS babies in Zaire will get some of this money."

"So will our seminaries who train future church leaders.

"We ask you to follow the flow of this money and to use it to speed the coming of Christ. Amen."

Murielle advanced the PowerPoint. "Here an example of another offering prayer you can use."

"(Lift the offering plates toward heaven) No matter what we say or do, this, o Lord, is what we think of you."

Even Murielle laughed. "You might get away with that prayer . . . once! The point is we can do much to improve the quality of worship around the offering experience. It is a chance to state our convictions about stewardship, to be reminded of God's great gift to us, and to demonstrate the dedication of what is most precious in our culture.

"Okay number twos. Your minute begins now!"

"That's me," Peter Connor said. "Money in our church is a constant problem. I almost have anxiety attacks whenever we start putting together our church budget. Every year people complain that the mission board wants more money, or that my salary kept pace with inflation, or that the church college is mismanaged. I learned long ago these complainers are blowing steam. They are not interested in a serious conversation about the economics of nonprofit institutions. They like to gripe, and our church environment allows it.

"For a long time I wondered how to create excitement about participating in ministry, rather than complaining. I don't know if dedicating offerings makes the difference. It certainly can't hurt."

Initiative Three-Strengthening a Ministry of Mercy

Murielle broke into the conversation again. "The first two initiatives were of the tuning and tweaking variety. Equipping pastors to do better stewardship education is relatively harmless, and the congregation will respond positively if they can connect sermons to the life they live Monday through Saturday. The congregation will also like a worship service with a bit more vigor and creativity in it, especially if they feel a deeper connection to God. But the remaining five initiatives are more difficult. Here is number three: strengthening a ministry of mercy.

"Luke records the story of the first deacons in Acts 6. They were appointed to oversee distribution of charity to widows in the Christian community. Deacons were appointed because the apostles, the pastors of the church in that day, could not perform ministries of mercy and fulfill their responsibilities for prayer and scriptural instruction. A similar problem occurs today when pastors are

expected to be the key ministers of mercy in congregational life, forcing them out of their important role of shepherding.

"Some churches do not expect the pastor to do all of the mercy ministry, so they appoint a benevolence committee whose responsibilities include helping people in need. This strategy is little better than expecting the pastor to do it, because response to crisis is slowed by a bureaucracy, and the inviting warmth of personal relationship gets watered down.

"Also, the word 'deacon' has come to mean different things to different congregations. Rather than use the word 'deacon, ' The Giving Project asks the church to be certain congregational mercy ministry is firmly in place. Our strategy is for congregations to appoint key members as eyes and ears for the church. Their job is to identify needs and link them to available resources, inviting other

congregational members to participate in mercy ministry. These point people are also networked with mutual aid societies, financial planners, church treasurers, and pastors as additional resources. The Giving Project provides training resources for people involved in mercy ministry.

"Let's say a young woman, fresh out of college, accepted a teaching job at one of the community schools. She rents an apartment and sets up her first household as a single adult. The church's 'mercy minister' organizes a household dedication service, and arranges for the young woman to meet with someone to answer questions she might have about being a faithful steward of her income, her talents, and her time. This could be one of the gentle nudges toward faithfulness the church can give its members throughout life's stages. It can also be the substance of mercy ministry to people in need.

"Number threes, you have a minute to respond."

Glenda waved her number three in the air. "It seems like Murielle's talking about less bureaucracy and more action when it comes to ministering mercy. I know I could use more help at Suburban Community. I'm the only staff person in a 125-member congregation. Some Sundays I'm almost embarrassed at the lack of preparation in my sermon, all because of the three to five emergencies I handled that week."

Initiative Four-Develop Relationships Between Gift Giver and Gift Receiver

Murielle broke in yet again. "It's no secret that people have become quite concerned about where donated dollars go. The unrighteous part of this concern is when people talk about giving their money, forgetting that all of life is dedicated to God. The righteous part of the concern isn't selfish, however. With all the scandals among television evangelists, and fundraising scams, people are more concerned than ever that their offerings really do honor God. So they try to keep those offerings close to home, where they can watch and see that the money gets used for its intended purposes. Here is an example of an alternative strategy to link giver and receiver:

"Instead of trying to get their minds and hearts around the entire planet, Hindleburg Fellowship decided to adopt Malaysia as their mission field. From input from the mission board of their denomination, they calculated their missions giving supported three-fourths of one missionary family serving in Malaysia. The missionary family will be on furlough next year. Instead of spending their furlough on the road in deputation work, the family will spend significant time at Hindleburg Fellowship doing mission education, substituting for Hindleburg's pastor who is going on sabbatical, and tooling up for their next term in Malaysia.

"In addition, Hindleburg sends someone from the congregation to Malaysia every other year to participate in the mission work and to bring back a report. On the odd year, someone from Malaysia comes to Hindleburg—sometimes an exchange student, or even a visiting pastor.

"Connections between gift givers and gift receivers can be made on a local scale as well. The previous initiative, strengthening mercy ministry, is one example. When a person extends mercy to a needy person, a more profound bond is created than when mercy is extended by a committee. We try to put human faces on the dollars contributed by the congregation.

"Number fours, you're on."

Franklin Warner-Seabolt spoke up. "This initiative sounds real good, and I think our congregation would respond well. Faith Fellowship gives about $15,000 a year to worldwide missions. I'm not sure how much it costs to put a family on the mission field, but if $15,000 was one-third the cost, theoretically we could have access to one-third of the missionary family's time when they are on furlough. We would get more intensive exposure to missions and the missionary family would not have to spread themselves so thin."

Franklin suddenly sat up with an inspired look on his face. "You know, it would be great if our church could connect in a direct way to Laos! We have several refugee families from there already as part of our congregation. This sort of thing might help the Caucasian members of our church get more involved in the refugee families' concerns, and ultimately help them feel a full part of our congregation!"

Initiative Five-Offering a Firstfruits Response

After a short break, Murielle moved on to initiative number five—offering a firstfruits response. "Everyone wants to know how much a tithe is. Should it be 10 percent of income? If so, should it be 10 percent of the gross or net income? We get even nit-pickier when we try to find out the exact number of pennies God needs in order to be satisfied.

"Rather than trying to nail down the exact amount of a tithe, The Giving Project moves the congregation through a series of retreats where participants identify the first and best that belongs to God. We start with the spiritual leadership of the church—the pastor, elders, the "deacons," *and* their spouses. They write a money autobiography and seek God's direction for the gifts they offer to God. This is the stone thrown into the pond-we want to send out large ripples into the congregation. These leaders then work with us to host additional retreats until at least 75 percent of the membership participates.

"We recommend your congregation host a workshop that connects planned giving to the Old Testament Jubilee celebrations. We also provide resources for your congregation to study the Christian belief system about money I identified earlier in my talk.

"This is the most comprehensive and difficult initiative to pull off. It is also the one most likely to bring spiritual renewal to your congregation.

"Number fives, it's your turn to respond."

Katy Warner-Seabolt signaled she was number five. "This initiative is the most difficult one for me to accept," she said. "Mrs. Yoder says it brings spiritual renewal—but I want to know how. Not that I doubt the truthfulness of her statements, but what she's describing is a massive undertaking. If the informal, extended family that dominates all the major positions of our church is going to embrace a formal, specific process like this one, then I want to be sure it is worth it before I even whisper the idea to any of our church leadership."

Initiative Six-Effective Leadership Transition

Murielle called everyone back to attention. "Much of our leadership transition is ineffective. The generation in power is reluctant to share power with people new to the faith. Some newcomers leave in discouragement when it becomes clear the church does not belong to them, but to those who built and currently police it. Others find a congregation that allows them access to church decisions. Those who stick it out bide their time until those who are in control fade from the scene. Either way the newcomer and the young person end up becoming the next generation of power abusers—seeking to protect that which they waited so long to create, rather than rallying the congregation around God's vision.

"Here's a true story with names and some details changed to protect privacy: Downtown Believers' Church was planted in 1946, just after World War II, when a number of newly 'liberated' young men married and discovered their world travels made it difficult to settle back on the old family farm. This church was born with a strong emphasis on gospel hymns, church bands, and a fairly consistent pattern of worship with the sermon always at the end.

"Twenty-five years later, the children of this congregation wanted different music and less formal worship. Some charismatic influences were finding their way in. The older generation balked at 'devil music' or jeans in church. The church board even passed a policy that men with uncut hair could not sing in the choir or sit on the platform.

"The young people of the church soon left and formed Suburban Fellowship, a congregation that blessed informality. They did away with membership, used accompaniment track tapes for special music whenever they felt like it, refused to purchase an organ, and let people attend in blue jeans or shorts.

"Another 25 years passed. Suburban Fellowship recently split also. Young people and newcomers wanted a Saturday night service as a means of outreach. The church said no because on Saturday night a number of twelve-step programs met in the church building. Many of Suburban's young people were more interested in 'hanging together' with their church friends than participating in the highly structured program ministries that had evolved over the years. A small group of young people investigated the possibility of hosting a Saturday church service in another congregation's facilities. Downtown Believers church, of all places, welcomed them with open arms. What had once been a thriving congregation had dwindled to a dozen senior citizens who no longer cared about anything except keeping the church doors open. Now the old church building has a new name and a new coat of paint. Downtown Peace Fellowship hosts a Saturday night coffee bar complete with poetry readings, and Sunday afternoon services have begun. Some of those senior citizens from the old Downtown church are the biggest financial supporters of this fledgling congregation."

Murielle paused. "Friends, it doesn't have to be this way. We can practice discipleship with far greater effectiveness than in this case study. The Giving Project helps congregations improve assimilation of new members, paying special attention to the ministry of hospitality. We help churches build leadership cultivation into the fabric of congregational life. We promote respect between generations. To summarize: Those in leadership positions have not really led until they have successfully trained someone to fill their shoes. Congregations that want to develop a community of committed, dedicated, and generous Christians know how important it is to develop the next generation of Christianity."

Murielle gestured toward the tables. "Those of you with the number six-get started."

"Whew!" said Andrew Jones. "This initiative leaves me panting for air . . . and wanting to hear more! Beulah Church is the only church I've known in 36 years of pastoral ministry. Twice during that time we saw significant groups of people leave—the most recent just five years ago. Each time they said they wanted to attend somewhere they felt more useful. I never could accept that as the reason."

Andrew grew more sober. "Now I wonder if some of the issues that Murielle Yoder identified weren't at play during those days. I'd like to retire in a couple of years, but I can't say as I've helped prepare anyone to take over the spiritual leadership of my flock."

Initiative Seven-Improve Congregational Financial Management

Murielle cut in for a final time. "Here is a list for improving congregational financial management. *First,* some congregations need to train their people in good committee process. The kinks in any congregational system seem to show up when the church discusses money and what church committee doesn't discuss money? Fix the decision-making system first, so that important monetary decisions can be made effectively. *Second,* congregations working with The Giving Project will be asked to establish a congregational mission statement with clear goals. *Third,* we help churches establish a yearly process that builds ownership for a congregation's financial commitments. This includes establishing a reserve fund, putting together spending ratios to guide the planning process, committing to a percentage of giving outside the congregation, and inviting the congregation to estimate their giving on an annual basis. By working with these tools, and hooking the congregation's mission to proactive financial planning, a church starts to fund a ministry they look forward to rather than funding last year's program all over again.

"There are some structural things that assist congregational financial planning as well. We recommend all new church programs be given a charter, going through in-depth reviews every three to five years. We also recommend churches go to a moderator—elect, moderator, and past-moderator structure on whatever they call their executive board or church council.

"It's your turn, number sevens. "

"That's me," Charley Harness said. "I think two things Mrs. Yoder mentioned would be of help to Chosen Community Fellowship, although I admit I'm stumped as to how to begin working at them. "The first thing is we could sure use some help with our church board and several of our committees. It seems like most of the time we can't come to a decision, and when we do—like our decision to let only men be ushers—someone goes home offended. There has to be a better way.

"The second thing is that all the churches I've pastored robbed their missions giving to make sure the electric bill got paid whenever there was a shortfall. I never felt right about that. Here I was asking church members to give from their first and best, like Mrs. Yoder said, but as a congregation we did just the opposite. I'd like to hear more about strategies to get away from that."

Wrap-up

"First, your congregation is a system, an intricate web of relationships," Murielle said. "Introduce one change and the system changes. The Giving Project can help you steer that system in a positive direction, paying attention to the careful cultivation required if you want to build a community of generous stewards for the long term.

"Second, it's difficult to talk about one of these congregational initiatives separate from the others. Start working with better congregational financial planning and you get into leadership development. Start developing leaders and you have to work at congregational vision. Address congregational vision and you need to think about links between gift giver and gift receiver. That is why we don't recommend implementing just part of this system, and ignoring the others. It is virtually impossible to do."

Suggestions

a. Evaluate t he preaching and teaching about Christians and money in your congregation. What money messages do you remember? Does the pastor bring them or is someone else expected to do it? Does the way your congregation talks about money reflect a sensitivity to economic differences? Do the people entrusted with the spiritual maturity of the congregation have access to information of whether people are giving or not?

b. Consider the methods your church uses to receive an offering. Do your methods mirror any of those described at the beginning of the chapter? Does your church dedicate the money offered to God? Is the offering a central act of worship?

c. What kind of mercy does your congregation show in comparison to the list found in Matthew 25:31-46? Who is responsible for it? Are those people able to call on you for assistance in any way, or are they pretty much on their own? How could your congregation become more effective in demonstrating mercy, especially with the financial resources of your congregation?

d. Work through the following five questions about links between gift giver and gift receiver. (1) Do you know any of the people on the receiving end of your congregation's benevolent offerings? (2) Do you have regular contact with missionaries your church dollar supports? (3) When was the last time a Christian from another country had occasion to speak in your worship service? (4) What kind of exposure did they get? (5) How long has it been since your church sent anyone overseas for a missions visit, particularly someone new to the faith or a young adult?

e. Evaluate your personal firstfruits response. Do you give the first and best of your income to God? Do you manage the rest in ways that give glory to God? Take a minute to sketch out the main points of your money autobiography were you to write one. (A money autobiography is your life story around money. It is surprisingly easy to write.) Start with these two questions: What messages did your parents send you about money, and how did you live them out?

f. Talk to the young people and newcomers in your congregation. What percentage of the congregation do they represent? Do they feel the congregation allows them to help shape congregational life? Do they feel they are being mentored? Has anyone blessed them to take part in ministry? Do they feel their gifts are being used in service to Christ?

g. Take stock of your congregational financial management. How is your church at making decisions? Is improvement needed? Does your church have a compelling sense of why God wants them here for such a time as this, and do they seek to fund God's wishes accordingly? In other words, does the plan for spending line up with the vision? Do you pay attention to ratios for distribution? Does your congregation have a reserve fund? Are church members familiar with planned giving resources?

Appendix 1

How to Lead Groups Through This Book

ANYONE WHO TEACHES THIS material will need to keep in mind one of three basic scenarios:

1. A group committed to serious study.

Such a group will read the book ahead of time, be fairly articulate about their study, and will participate to a high degree. If this is the case, they can adequately cover the material at the pace of a chapter a week. The class structure could include (a) the teacher briefly summarizing the material, (b) time for some discussion about the biblical perspective and the many reflection scenarios, and (c) time to work at one or more of the suggestions at the end of each chapter.

2. A class that is not likely to read the book in advance.

If this is the case, consider this book your teacher's guide rather than a student manual. Slow the pace of the class by dividing each chapter into these three sections:

  a. Biblical input—Prepare a lecture or interactive Bible study based on the passages used in each chapter.

b. Discussion—Work with the reflection scenarios in each chapter.

c. Application—Follow through on some of the suggestions. at the end of each chapter. This approach requires a flexible time frame. Some chapters may need to be spread across as many as three weeks.

3. A class that is a mix of 1 and 2.

IF YOU HAVE BOTH serious and casual students, act as a facilitator for the discussions, a style that lets you bring out the biblical material without intimidating those who do not prepare. Move back and forth between asking people to summarize their reading and inviting everyone to talk about their thoughts. Again, plan for adequate time to work with both the reflection scenarios and the suggestions.

An alternative is to plan a short-term discussion group for interested people. Regular class time could be given to shorter sections of biblical summary, reflection, and working with the suggestions. The discussion group could take any one of the three to greater depth.

Please note: The reflection scenarios (case studies) are particularly effective at helping Christians express their convictions about money in the presence of their sisters and brothers. If you do nothing else, make use of these case studies. For additional reflection scenarios, see Appendix 2.

Appendix 2 —————————————————————

On Further Reflection . . .

MONEY DECISIONS ARE COMPLEX. The following case studies help us bring our money difficulties into the open. When we keep money in the private realm and avoid the complexity of economic situations, we are more apt to criticize our Christian brothers and sisters. When we know their stories, and the difficult choices they face, we are more ready to discuss economic realities with compassion. If you enjoyed the discussions these case studies can generate, here are a few additional ones. How would you counsel these people?

This world keeps putting us in mucky situations where we must choose the best option, knowing some inherent evil keeps getting attached. We mourn what is wrong. We celebrate what is right. We admit we can always do better. Philip Yancey, a well-known Christian writer echoed these sentiments:

> "I began to see that biblical principles on justice and equality have to be worked out in a real world of economics. And in that world, does reduced consumption indeed help the world's problems? What would happen if all American Christians, out of concern for the world's inequities, altered their consumption patterns? We saw an indication in the oil crisis of the 70s: After enduring justified criticism for our voracious oil appetite, we cut imports dramatically. In the process we almost wrecked the economies of Nigeria and Mexico. We could cut coffee

drinking in half, but economies in Brazil and Kenya and much of Latin America would go into a tailspin."[1]

a. Peter Hoffmann is a college financial aid counselor and committed Christian. Recently his supervisor instructed him to withhold maximum financial aid from students eager to attend the school, and to offer larger financial aid to students sitting on the fence, particularly to those interested in majors needing additional students. So, instead of seeking the student's interest Peter now feels like he sells cars. In addition, Peter grows more uncomfortable with the large aid packages given to student athletes, and the much more modest packages available to students training for public service jobs.

b. Joyful Community Church is located near a rest stop on the toll road. On each of the major holidays various fellowship groups from the congregation provide free coffee for travelers at the toll plaza. Although donations are welcome, the church uses this as an act of service only. No formal evangelism takes place. If it did the toll road officials would not let them provide the coffee. For the first three years of providing this service, Joyful Community was seen as an innovative and service-oriented congregation. Now the society for the blind put many of their people into business servicing vending machines at places like the toll plazas. The holiday season with its many travelers provides a significant percentage of their vending income. When organizations set up free coffee stands, it takes a big bite out of the incomes of these blind entrepreneurs. The society of the blind has publicly complained.

c. Fred Ludington made a mere $10,000 profit on his crops last year. He and his wife, Jenny, were committed to give $2,000 to their church, and they scrimped and saved to honor that pledge. But today Fred sold his corn at an unprecedented price. Fred conservatively estimates he will make $150,000

---

1. Money: *Confronting the Power of a Modern Idol*, Multnomah Press, 1985, 9.

over expenses. Although Fred's equipment should be good for some years yet, he still owes $500,000 on his land. Fred and Jenny gave sacrificially to the church. They gave on faith the income would come. Now there is a bounty. Fred and Jenny wonder what would please God the most-reducing indebtedness as fast as possible, or giving a firstfruits gift to the church.

d. Millie Solloway works at the grill in a downtown diner, making minimum wage for her thirty hours of work each week. No taxes are taken out and Millie receives no paid benefits. Millie doesn't have a lot of economic needs. She shares a small apartment with a roommate and walks to work and church. Each day after work, Millie pours herself a cup of coffee and reads the various newspapers left by the diner's patrons. Today she read about the huge gap between the income taxes the government expects to collect and the amount that actually comes in. The article gave an in-depth analysis of the underground cash economy that goes unreported, especially among small businesses like the diner Millie works for. Millie isn't an expert at math or with arguments over principle, but she has a strong sense of right and wrong. She worries whether she is guilty of participating in something illegal.

e. Sara Mills is pastor of Bridgewater Church, sometimes called First Church of Hamilton Plastics because so many people from Hamilton Plastics Incorporated are members. The church has a large endowment it uses to spruce up the building and grounds. Much of this endowment is invested in Hamilton Plastics stock. This year stock shot up and the church earned a huge dividend. The stock rose so high because Ernie Hamilton, CEO of Hamilton Plastics and lead bass in the church choir, took the company through a major corporate downsizing. Stockholders were pleased, but three church members just lost their jobs. Sara wonders what it means for a church to add to its endowment at the expense of church members' incomes. She also wonders about how these economic decisions will affect church relationships.

f. Guy Prybo is a new Christian who really wants to please God. He has lain awake the past couple of nights wondering about his job at the convenience store. Although there are gasoline pumps out front and banking services and grocery items offered inside, Guy knows a significant percentage of his hourly wage comes from the sale of tobacco, alcohol, lottery tickets, and pornographic magazines. Guy wonders what business a Christian has selling these things.

g. Perry and Susan Clinton have owned a lakeside cottage for fifteen years. They have always been generous to the church and community. They have given 10 percent of their income directly to their local congregation and contributed to a couple of community youth organizations on top of that. Perry even served on one ministry board when their oldest son became a teenager. Now their cottage is in need of significant repair. A storm tore off the northwest corner of the roof, just two days after they discovered their septic system was leaking into their neighbor's property. To make matters worse, they had let their property insurance lapse. The costs for replacement are so much, they probably won't be able to give at the same rate in the next calendar year. Both Perry and Susan feel guilty about this and wonder who they should talk to.

h. Paul Neufeld works at the steel mill in town. It's hard work, but he's thankful for the seniority he has built up over the years that saved him from the latest round of layoffs. His children are now grown, with one still in college. Between his work and his wife Anna's part-time job, they have enough to make ends meet and to make a modest contribution to their child's remaining year of college. But management and union talks are underway, with little hope for a new agreement. Management wants major wage concessions and the union wants a major wage and benefit increase. The union talks about a lengthy strike if their demands are not met. Paul wants to be sure his response is rooted in love for his God, his family, and his community.

i. Byron Porter, a Christian, lives next door to Phan Thangkanh, a Buddhist. Phan is Mister Super Neighbor, always helping whenever a home-improvement project is underway in the neighborhood. A structural engineer, Phan claims this sort of hands-on work is one way he tunes out the pressures of work. Two years ago, high winds blew the roof off of Byron's utility shed. Phan was there by evening, helping to put a new roof on. He also donated plastic sheeting to cover up unfinished sections for protection during the night. Now vandals climbed the wall of Phan's backyard and destroyed a grotto Phan had built as a place for meditation and prayer. Byron hears a knock on his door, answers, and finds the neighborhood association on his doorstep. They are taking a collection to help Phan rebuild the grotto. There is also a sign-up sheet to donate time to the project. As Byron was one of the many neighbors helped by Phan, certainly he would be willing to contribute, wouldn't he?

j. Jane Tampolo, a retired teacher, spends her days reading and tending the roses she and husband, Tyler, love. They have struck up a friendship with their new neighbor, a recently divorced and financially struggling investment broker named Melissa. The Tampolos have a $10,000 certificate of deposit coming due and they are thinking of purchasing an annuity. Melissa sent Jane a prospectus after a backyard fence conversation about it. The Tampolos also have an opportunity to set up a trust with their church foundation. Jane and Tyler enjoy their relationship with Melissa and want to invite her to their church. They are also longtime supporters of their church mission board. This feels to the Tampolos like a choice between investing in evangelism or demonstrating their loyalty to the church.

k. Howie Sanders, single father of three, is a new Christian. Last year his wife left her "lifeless spouse" for someone she found a little more exciting. She willingly gave up custody of the children and maxed out their five joint credit cards before leaving. Now Howie is on the verge of bankruptcy and the bank has foreclosed on their home. Creditors are leaving threatening messages on his voicemail by the hour and his parents made it clear that they cannot and will not bail him out, except to watch the kids from time to time.

l. Charity Pierce became a Christian eight years into her marriage. That was fifteen years ago. Her husband made it clear from the beginning he wanted none of his hard earned income lining the pockets of those money-grubbing preachers. At first, Charity sneaked some of her grocery money into the offering, but she felt too guilty about this deception to make it a habit. Her last child moved out of the house this year and she just accepted a secretarial position at the dealership. Now she is struggling how to manage this new income stream. She wants to start giving to her church and the youth drop-in center where she volunteers, but she knows how threatening it will be to her husband if she seeks full control of her income.

m. Jennifer Loepper had just returned to her prairie wheat farm from the co-op. She finished putting her supplies away, and decided to look at the receipt one more time before putting it in their expense file. She realized she had been given five dollars extra in change than was due her. Her strongest impulse is to return the money immediately, but it is a thirty-mile round trip to do so. And didn't she just read a news report that stores like the co-op had enough computer glitches in the pricing structure that she was being overcharged about 10 percent of the time anyway?

Appendix 3 _____

Summary Statements of Christian Beliefs about Money

Introduction

WE LIVE IN A consumer-minded culture. Our culture insists that we think about money—how we will earn it, how we will spend it, and whether we have enough of it. Since money is such a dominant force in our lives, as disciples of Jesus our faithfulness includes the actions we take with money. This is why Christians need a statement of beliefs about money.

A view of money

Because money has a godlike strength, our earning and use of money communicate our values.[1] Christians are called to share God's values-that is, to view and respond to creation the way God does. God's values include wanting to live with his people in a perfect society that he provides.[2] Christians, then, are citizens of the society God is building and are called to be loyal to its values. Our joyful response is to give our life's work to God's service, and to use wealth in cooperation with God's values.[3]

1. 1 Timothy 6:3-10.
2. Genesis 1-3; Deuteronomy 11; 28; Isaiah 65:17-25; Revelation 5; 21; 22.
3. Titus 3:3-8; Luke 6:27-35; Matthew 5:45; Exodus 20:22-23:33; Deuteronomy 12-16; Leviticus 17-26; Matthew 25:31-46.

As Christians practice their beliefs about money, they must remember that God accomplishes his saving work through Jesus, the Christ and Lord of the universe.[4] When we joyfully meet God's grace in Jesus, we are empowered to live out our belief that God is Owner of all. We dedicate all of life in an act of worship to God. We commit ourselves to participate in God's saving work.[5] We show this dedication when we give back to God' out of the first and best of the resources we manage on God's behalf, and by managing the rest in generous ways that give glory to God.[6]

When we make decisions about generous and grace-filled living, we are helped by seeking the guidance of the Holy Spirit and the counsel of the church—our family of greatest importance.[7]

4. Colossians 1:15-20; Philippians 3:8; Revelation 5.

5. Matthew 19:29; 1 Corinthians 4:8-13;James 4:1-10; Romans 12:1, 2; 1 Peter 2:9, 10; Revelation 5.

6. Genesis 17; Deuteronomy 14; 15; 26; Leviticus 23; Numbers 8; 18; Matthew 23:23; 1 Corinthians 16:1-4;2 Corinthians 8:1-3; Ephesians 1:3-14; James 2:14-17, 27.

7. A~ts 4:32-5:7; 2 Corinthians 8:1-15; Galatians 6: 1-5; 1 Timothy 6:11-16; 2 Timothy 4:1-5.

Appendix 4

Article 21, Christian Stewardship

Statement from the Confession of Faith in a Mennonite Perspective Article 21-Christian Stewardship—Reprinted from Confession of Faith in a Mennonite Perspective, pp. 77-80. Copyright © 1995, Herald Press, Scottdale, Pa. Used by permission.

WE BELIEVE THAT EVERYTHING belongs to God, who calls us as the church to live as faithful stewards of all that God has entrusted to us.

As servants of God, our primary vocation is to be stewards in God's household.[1] God, who in Christ has given us new life, has also given us spiritual gifts to use for the church's nurture and mission.[2] The message of reconciliation has been entrusted to every believer, so that through the church the mystery of the gospel might be made known to the world.[3]

We believe that time also belongs to God and that we are to use with care the time of which we are stewards.[4] Yet, from earliest days, the people of God have been called to observe special periods of rest and worship. In the Old Testament, the seventh day was holy because it was the day God rested from the work

---

1. Luke 12:35-48; 1 Corinthians 4:1-2.
2. 1 Peter 4:10-11; Titus 1:6; 2:5.
3. 2 Corinthians 5:10-20; Ephesians 3:1-10.
4. Psalms 31:15; Ephesians 5:15-16; Colossians 4:5.

of creation.[5] The Sabbath was also holy because of God's deliverance of the Hebrew people from slavery.[6] Through Jesus, all time is holy, set apart for God and intended to be used for salvation, healing, andjustice.[7] In the present time, the church celebrates a day of holy rest, commonly the first day of the week, and is called to live according to Sabbath justice at all times.

We acknowledge that God as Creator is Owner of all things. In the Old Testament, the Sabbath year and the Jubilee year were practical expressions of the belief that the land is God's and the people of Israel belong to God.[8] Jesus, at the beginning of his ministry, announced the year of the Lord's favor, often identified with Jubilee. Through Jesus, the poor heard good news, captives were released, the blind saw, and the oppressed went free.[9] The first church in Jerusalem put Jubilee into practice by preaching the gospel, healing the sick, and sharing possessions. Other early churches shared financially with those in need.[10]

As stewards of God's earth, we are called to care for the earth and to bring rest and renewal to the land and everything that lives on it.[11] As stewards of money and possessions, we are to live simply, practice mutual aid within the church, uphold economic justice, and give generously and cheerfully.[12] As persons dependent on God's providence, we are not to be anxious about the necessities of life, but to seek first the kingdom of God.[13] We cannot be true servants of God and let our lives be ruled by desire for wealth.

We are called to be stewards in the household of God, set apart for the service of God. We live out now the rest and justice

5. Exodus 20:8-11.
6. Deuteronomy 5:12-15.
7. Mark 2:27-28.
8. Leviticus 25:23, 42, 55.
9. Luke 4:16-21.
10. Acts 2:44-45; 4:32-37; 2 Corinthians 8:10-15.
11. Psalms 24:1; Genesis 1:26-28.
12. Philemon 4:11-12; 2 Corinthians 8:13-14; James 5:4; 2 Corinthians 9:7.
13. Matthew 6:24-33.

which God has promised.[14] The church does this while looking forward to the coming of our Master and the restoration of all things in the new heaven and new earth.

Commentary

1. The word *stewardship* in the New Testament is used primarily in connection with stewardship of the gospel. But in the broader sense, stewardship is related to the idea of God as Head of the household, in which Christians are God's servants or managers or sons and daughters entrusted with responsibility. First-century households acted as economic units and often included people not biologically related. Thus, the term stewardship has come to refer to our responsibility both for sharing the gospel and for managing time, material things, and money.

2. Our tradition of simple living is rooted not in frugality for its own sake, but in dependence on God, the Owner of everything, for our material needs. We depend on God's gracious gifts for food and clothing, for our salvation, and for life itself. We do not need to hold on tight to money and possessions, but can share what God has given us. The practice of mutual aid is a part of sharing God's gifts so that no one in the family of faith will be without the necessities of life. Whether through community of goods or other forms of financial sharing, mutual aid continues the practice of Israel in giving special care to widows, orphans, aliens, and others in economic need (Deuteronomy 24: 17-22). Tithes and firstfruit offerings were also a part of this economic sharing (Deuteronomy 26; compare Matthew 23:23).

3. Economic justice is an integral part of the Sabbath cycle. The Sabbath year, like the Sabbath day, brought rest and freedom for the land and for laborers. The seven-times seventh year or the fiftieth year, the year of Jubilee, also brought justice

14. Matthew 11:28-29; Revelation. 7:15-] 7.

and mercy by the return of family land, release of debts, and freedom for bound laborers (Leviticus 25). The effect of the Sabbath-Jubilee laws was a return to relative economic equality every fifty years. Jesus taught his disciples to pray, "Forgive us our debts, as we also have forgiven our debtors" (Matthew 6: 12). In the age to come, the saints will have the economic necessities (Revelation 7:15-17). We are to seek first the reign of God and to cease from consumerism, unchecked competition, overburdened productivity, greed, and possessiveness.

4. Not only was the Sabbath observed in Old Testament times; there is evidence that the sabbatical year and the year of Jubilee were also observed. Jubilee law appears in Leviticus 25; Leviticus 27:16-25; and Numbers 36:4. Other references to sabbatical or Jubilee years occur in Deuteronomy 31:10; 2 Chronicles 36:21; Isaiah 37:30; 61:1-2; Jeremiah 34:8-22; and Ezekiel 46:17. The first-century Jewish historian, Josephus, refers to a time when the Jews in Palestine went hungry because of a sabbatical or Jubilee year, when the land lay fallow. The Roman government exempted Judea from tribute during the seventh year. The practice of the Jerusalem church and the continued financial sharing of Christian congregations is evidence that the economic aspects of Jubilee continued to be practiced and adapted to urban settings.

5. The theology of stewardship makes us aware not only of care for human beings, but of care for the rest of creation. Animals and fields benefited from the Sabbath and the sabbatical year. An observance of Sabbath: Jubilee calls us to take care of and preserve the earth. We are to commit ourselves to right use of the earth 's resources as a way of living now according to the model of the new heaven and the new earth.

Appendix 5 _____

More Reasons Money has a God-like Power[1]

MY WORK PROVIDES OPPORTUNITY to talk to many people about money. Some people tell me they hate it. They hate what they have seen it do to others and to themselves. They don't want the number of victims to grow. They wish life would not be so clouded by monetary concerns.

Others talk about the wonders of money. They are comfortable with living in the economy and unraveling money's secrets. They point to the positive results money can achieve-food, medicine, shelter, and entertainment. They feel affectionate toward money.

Both viewpoints are eclipsed by those who hold that money is amoral and neutral. That is, they believe money can either destroy or build depending on the intent of the user. But while this understanding better addresses the complications of money, it still falls short of fully addressing the latent, pulsing, god-like power that money has.

All three of these viewpoints recognize that power and money are linked. The first viewpoint fears money's power. The second *gives it too much* credence. The third thinks the individual who holds it is more powerful than the money itself. Unfortunately, none of these viewpoints recognize money's ability to

1. Revised and adapted from what originally published in *Stewards of New Life*, by the American Baptist Churches, 2003.

simultaneously serve God and compete with God, to help and to harm, to restore and destroy. Whether one has much or very little; whether one walks towards it or attempts to abandon it, the power of money is always present. We need a more sophisticated understanding still.

In chapter two of this book, I wrote of seven reasons why money has a god-like power (see sidebar). This appendix describes the eighth and ninth reason why money's power is so god-like. Together they begin to develop the more sophisticated understanding we seek.

7 reasons why money has a god-like power:

1. Money outlives you (It was here before you and lives after
2. you)
3. Money has a greater circle of influence than you do (It goes places you can't go and touches people you could not otherwise touch).
4. Money is mysterious (It cannot be fully described or understood).
5. Money lives in the realm of things we are tempted to worship (The first three reasons are characteristics of what humans normally worship).
6. Money mimics everything God promises in the New Jerusalem (It may be only temporary, but it is available now).
7. Money is something you wield (You swing it as scalpel or sword sometimes both at the same time. Doing so, you cannot control all the outcomes).
8. Everything can be monetized (All the wonderful and godly things we aspire to can be assigned an economic cost).

Reason #8: Money can make you think you are God.

With more money comes the feeling of control over one's circumstances and power to define reality. Call it *sovereignty*. Notice your level of irritation over the interference of others, the way their interruptions ruin your plans. Only those who believe they have the resources to control their circumstances suffer this problem.

With more money comes the ability to purchase and use technology. Technology allows for efficiency, increased production, an even greater income, and the possibility of becoming even more powerful through the use of new advances in technology. Call it *omnipotence*. The more I have the more I can do and the more rapidly I can do it.

Acquisition of technology also leads one to aspire to *omnipresence*, the feeling you can be everywhere and anywhere. Not too long ago I walked a residential street in Southern California, talking with three other people in Chicago, Rochester, New York and New York City. An hour later I was in another town presenting to pastors who came from up to ninety miles away. The next morning I attended a meeting in Atlanta. Technology makes geographic distance disappear.

An aspiration to *immanence* also becomes possible. So does a desire to be *omniscient*. Immanence is the quality of being near by—the opposite end of sovereignty. Witness the parents who rig video from the nursery to watch on their work computer terminal. They do this to monitor the quality of care their infant receives. They are far away, yet nearby. Omniscience- the quality of knowing everything—shows up in the way I use my smartphone—a computer more powerful than the first two computers I owned. It gives me instant access to the World Wide Web. I can monitor my investments, travel timetables, manage e-mail, remain up to date with the world's headlines, and look up information on all subjects. I can know whatever I need to know when I need to know it.

With more money comes the aspiration for perfection as well. Peter Mayle wrote of this in his work *Acquired Taste*.

"Expectations tend to increase in direct proportion to the amount of money being spent, and if you're spending a fortune you expect perfection. Alas, life being the badly organized shambles that it so often is, and with so much of it dependent on the behavior of erratic equipment (servants), perfection is rare. After a while, the rich realize this, and they start looking for trouble. I've seen them do it. Details that we would consider trivial assume enormous significance: the breakfast egg is inedible because it is marginally under boiled, the silk shirt is unwearable because of a barely visible wrinkle, the chauffer is insupportable because he's been eating garlic again, the doorman is either insufficiently attentive or overly familiar-the list of maddening blots on the landscape of life just goes on and on. How can you have a nice day if some fool hasn't warmed your socks or ironed your newspaper properly?"[2]

Access to vast amounts of money can also make us think we are a *benefactor*—in this case one who wins favor or becomes an *object of worship* by showing mercy to others. Being a benefactor has become the very heart of philanthropy—indeed the crux and crucible for the financial straits of North American Christianity. The giver ceases responding to God as an act of worship and now demands worship for the generosity they show. "Say 'thank you' for my magnanimity!'" they demand. "Etch my name in a plaque!" "Send me a book in thanks for my gift!" "Do what I demand, or else!"

Then there is being *eternal*. Access to money further breeds my desire for a legacy. I become concerned about the distribution of my estate, the size of my tomb, what history will make of me, that my children and grandchildren will do me honor. I chase the latest in science or folk medicine to extend my life. I pursue eternal youth through exercise, diet and cosmetic surgery.

Aspiring to be God, I become guilty of the very sin that cast Lucifer out of heaven. Can you imagine this state of affairs? Oh that we would only be worshipping the dollar sign! Then we could

2. Quoted in *The rich are different*, by Jon Winokur, Pantheon Books, 1996, 151, 152.

merely point to idolatry and invite people to repent. Instead we fill our pews with our ever-indulgent selves, expecting that the very life of the congregation must become a celebration of our personal preferences. This assumes chat we still attend, of course. Wealth has a way of moving us into our own temples of lake cottages, large motor homes, sailing vessels or carefully manicured lawns with eighteen precisely placed holes.

To be created in God's image is a gift from God. So is having eternity in our hearts. To use resources in partnership with God is right and good. To have access to many resources and to put them to use in service to God is a wonderful opportunity. However, we must recognize it as all too easy to turn these gifts from God toward our own selfish ends-to chink chat we are a replacement for God rather than a companion to God. So often we have understood the powerful draw of money as resting in money itself. The apostle Paul understood better. Read 1 Timothy 6 again and you will see him pressing the believer not to understand chat money is evil, but to understand chat money might lead them from the faith, enabling them to think they are, in fact, God.

It has been often said that a man who serves as is his own lawyer is a fool. We might say the same for anyone who concludes they are their own god.

Reason #9: Money has the power to transform a life[3]

It was a stockbroker and Lutheran church member that deepened my awareness that Money possesses significant transformational power. One can convert to the cause of money and order their life around it just as they would a Messiah. One simply does not interact with it and come away unchanged.

The Scriptures do not neglect this message of life-transforming events when dealing with material wealth. Jacob mistreated Esau in order to gain his birthright. King Ahab lusted over Naboch's vineyard and his wife orchestrated murder to get it for him.

3. Adapted from Depth Perception,© Design For Ministry'", December 2005.

Ananias and Sapphira manipulated their giving report to make themselves look more generous than they really were. Simon the Magician tried to purchase the gift of healing instead of understanding it as a special grace from God.

Not all money transformation was negative. We have biblical examples of the poor rejoicing in the Lord through the giving of others.

Zacchaeus delighted in his interaction with Jesus and vowed to give half of what he owned to the poor. He also pledged to lavishly repay any claims against him. Joseph of Arimethea donated property for the grave of his Lord. The apostle Paul used his tent making trade as a means to support his missionary journeys.

Having more or having less transforms one's perspective. Whether the transformation harms or helps is largely connected to whether a person is tapped into God's grace and has already been transformed by the renewing of their mind (Romans 12:1). Then a person can see money for what it is . . . and what it isn't.

Bibliography

Bellah, Robert N., et al. *Habits of the Heart: Individualism and Commitment in American Life*. Berkeley, CA: University of California Press, 1985.

Bosch, David J. *Believing in the Future*. Leominster, UK: Gracewing, 1995.

Brethren, Hutterian. *The Chronicle of Hutterian Bretheren*. Vol. 1. Walden, NY: Plough, 1986.

Bromily, Geoffrey W. *Gender and Grace*. Westmont, IL: InterVarsity, 1990.

Burkholder, J.R. "Money: Master or Servant?" Flushing, NY: Gospel Herald, 1974.

Confession of Faith in a Mennonite Perspective. Harisonburg, VA: Herald, 1995.

Forbush, William Byron, ed. *Fox's Book of Martyrs*. Grand Rapids, MI: Zondervan, 1967.

Getz, Gene. *A Biblical Theology of Material Possessions*. Chicago, IL: Moody, 1990.

Proceedings. Menonite Church General Assembly.

Koontz, Ted, ed. *Godward: Personal Stories of Grace*. Scottdale, PA: Herald, 1996.

Nola, Paulinus. *Ancient Christian Writers: The Poems of St. Paulinus of Nola*. Vol. 40. Newman, 1975.

Popov, Haralan. *Tortured for His Faith*. Grand Rapids, MI: Zondervan, 1970.

Redekop, Calvin, et al., eds. In *Anabaptist/Mennonite Faith and Economics*. Lanham, MD: University Press of America, 1994.

Schlabach, Gerald. *And Who is My Neighbor? Poverty, Privilege, and the Gospel of Christ*. Harrisonburg, VA: Herald, 1991.

Wenger, Grace A. *Stewards of the Gospel*. Harrisonburg, VA: Herald, 1964.